The Making of the 20th Century

This series of specially commissioned titles focuses attention on significant and often controversial events and themes of world history in the present century. Each book provides sufficient narrative and explanation for the newcomer to the subject while offering, for more advanced study, detailed source-references and bibliographies, together with interpretation and reassessment in the light of recent scholarship.

In the choice of subjects there is a balance between breadth in some spheres and detail in others; between the essentially political and matters economic or social. The series cannot be a comprehensive account of everything that has happened in the twentieth century, but it provides a guide to recent research and explains something of the times of extraordinary change and complexity in which we live. It is directed in the main to students of contemporary history and international relations, but includes titles which are of direct relevance to courses in economics, sociology, politics and geography.

The Making of the 20th Century

Series Editor: CHRISTOPHER THORNE

Titles in the Series include

Already published

The Illusion of Peace

International Relations in Europe 1918–1933

Sally Marks

St. Martin's Press   New York

*For Carl Hamilton Pegg,
a mentor to whom this
work owes much*

Contents

The illustration on the front of the jacket shows the representatives of the subscribing powers at the signing of the Treaty of Locarno at the Foreign Office, London, 1925. Reproduced with the permission of the Radio Times – Hulton Picture Library.

Acknowledgements

THE author acknowledges receipt of research time and research funds from Rhode Island College. She is also grateful to Beth Perry and Louise Sherby of the Adams Library for patient assistance in verifying references and tracking down details, and to the following colleagues, friends and students who have read and commented on portions of the text: Joan Goodman, Mary Lucas, Martha Scott, Tony Teng, Izabella Tereszczenko and Panajotis Votoras. Her warm thanks are due to Christopher Thorne for genuinely constructive editorial advice.

1 The Pursuit of Peace

MAJOR wars often provide the punctuation marks of history, primarily because they force drastic realignments in the relationships among states. To this rule the First World War was no exception. Long before the fighting ceased in November 1918, it was evident that the map of Europe must be redrawn and that reallocation of colonies, creation of a new international organisation, and changes in the economic balance must considerably affect the rest of the world as well. The First World War heralded the end of European dominance as the true victors in this predominantly European war were America and Japan: two non-European powers. The European victors were bled white and suffered a pyrrhic victory from which none of them ever really recovered. While this fact was not evident at the war's end, it was clear that the forthcoming settlement must far exceed in geographic scope and complexity those other periodic realignments of the power balance, the 1648 Treaty of Westphalia and the 1815 Final Act of Vienna, to which it is often compared. Nobody doubted the magnitude of the task ahead but nobody was properly prepared to undertake it.

As often happens the sudden collapse of the enemy took the victors by surprise. Germany had been expected to hold out until mid-1919 and, in the autumn of 1918, Allied energy was more concentrated upon winning the war than upon planning the peace. True, some planning was in progress, but not always in the most effectual quarters. In the final year of the war the smaller Allied states pursued their limited, specific aims with energy, but achieved only cautious and qualified commitments. Exile organisations representing ethnic groups within the Central Powers did the same with similar results. They recognised that the ultimate court of appeal would consist of Britain, France and America, but these three, who had the task of planning for much of the world, were also responsible for winning the war. Not surprisingly, that came first.

See wington
consequences
of
franco-prussian
war

Of the major Allies the French were perhaps the best organised in planning ahead, mainly because they knew precisely what mattered to them and because their interests were not really global. In London the Foreign Office was industriously preparing position papers on every conceivable topic, but, since its views often did not coincide with those of the Cabinet, and even less with those of Prime Minister David Lloyd George, much of the work proved futile.

In America the situation was more obscure. A special organisation called the Inquiry had been established late in 1917 under the supervision of the President's confidant, Edward M. House, to research the problems of the peace and to prepare a programme designed to pre-empt those of European leaders. The Inquiry, composed largely of academicians and functioning independently of the State Department, was hard at work, but its influence was still uncertain and House himself was in Paris during the closing weeks of the war.[1] Secretary of State Robert Lansing was preparing his views, which did not coincide with those of the Inquiry and which could be expected to clash with those of the President. As for Woodrow Wilson himself, so far as could be ascertained, the American President had no views beyond the hazy slogans of his Fourteen Points, enumerated as a peace programme in an address to Congress on 8 January 1918.[2] While these provided a splendid propaganda platform of high moral tone, they were too ambiguous to serve as the basis for a settlement.

Wilson's
+ moral
megalomania

When the Germans, recognising the advantages of ambiguity, suddenly on 4 October 1918 requested an armistice on the basis of the Fourteen Points, they addressed themselves to Wilson alone, and he negotiated unilaterally for nearly a month while the Allies watched nervously. In deference to the American tradition of isolationism and fear of 'entangling alliances', Wilson had insisted that America was not an Ally but rather an 'Associated Power', and Allied statesmen recognised that the distinction was appropriate. Despite some similarity in Wilson's and Lloyd George's public pronouncements, Allied leaders knew that America's war aims had little in common with theirs. France's chief concern was security *vis-à-vis* Germany. Italy and Japan wanted as much territory as possible at the expense of their neighbours, and the smaller states tended to be territorially ambitious as well. Britain cared mainly about restoration of the traditional balance of power and

all agree on financial debts to U.S

economic patterns on the continent, preservation of British naval supremacy, and enlargement of the Empire. These were time-honoured objectives, understood and acknowledged by European leaders. Yet America, to whom most states directly or indirectly owed enormous sums of money, had no territorial or economic claims and no financial demands beyond the substantial one of debt repayment, a burden to be levied on the victors, not on the foe. Furthermore, Allied leaders feared that Wilson was a genuine idealist and suspected he really believed his own rhetoric about 'permanent peace' and 'the world must be made safe for democracy'. They suspected as well that Wilson viewed himself as the Angel of the Lord, coming to deliver Europe from decadence and corruption, and they worried that the Fourteen Points, which no Allied leader had endorsed, might have become Holy Writ in Wilson's eyes. Above all, as October 1918 progressed, they feared that he might still be imbued with the 'peace without victory' sentiments he had uttered before America's entry into the war, and fretted that Wilson was probably giving too much away to Germany as he negotiated alone.

While Allied assessments of Wilson were accurate in some respects, the fears about Germany were groundless. He had given nothing away before the Allies were brought into the negotiations late in October. Allied leaders in Paris, together with House, hastily settled the terms. The chief Allied concern was to ensure that the Armistice was in fact a surrender and that Germany could not resume hostilities. This was achieved by draconian military terms which required rapid German withdrawal behind the Rhine (and which had the unanticipated effect of tightening the German army's grip on the nascent Weimar republic).[3] The chief American concern was to ensure the inclusion of Wilson's Fourteen Points and his subsequent pronouncements, some of which were contradictory,[4] to serve as the basis for the peace. Despite much reinterpretation and one British reservation on freedom of the seas, this also was achieved.[5] After Germany accepted the terms on 11 November 1918 and the guns fell silent on the western front, the victors set about planning for an Allied peace conference to be followed, they assumed, by a peace congress with Germany and the other defeated Central Powers.

At this juncture, administrative chaos set in. The French had insisted upon Paris as the site of the conference, but it was a poor

see Levin by Spruce p. 78

administrative chaos

choice. Not only did wartime passions run higher there than in any other likely location but, after four years of the strains of war, the French capital was in no condition to provide hotel rooms, offices, limousines, printing presses, and the myriad other facilities required by the untold thousands of delegates, experts, clerks and newsmen pouring into Paris. Wilson, delayed by the opening of Congress and by the Atlantic crossing, arrived in mid-December to find nothing prepared. Britain and France had not even named their delegates. Statesmen who needed to contemplate the problems ahead were instead coping with a ceaseless flow of querulous complaints about room allocations, despatch boxes, and all the administrative trivia essential to the functioning of so large a conference. The confusion in Paris before and during the deliberations was almost indescribable and contributed considerably to the erratic course of events.

The problems facing the peacemakers were staggering in their magnitude and compounded by a bewildering array of wartime promises, pronouncements, and treaty commitments. The range of agreement among the Allied and Associated Powers was narrow. It was established that all Allied territories occupied by the enemy should be evacuated and restored, but there was no real agreement on what 'restoration' encompassed. It was understood that France would receive Alsace-Lorraine without a plebiscite, that Belgium's territorial and legal status would be improved, and that Poland would be re-created, although its location and size remained uncertain. Until the Armistice, there was also an agreed ambiguity about the future of the Habsburg Empire. Despite constant *émigré* pressure, particularly from the Czechs,[6] Allied and American pronouncements had been vague because, almost to the end, Allied leaders hoped for a separate peace with Austria–Hungary and were prepared to subordinate national self-determination to that aim.

Beyond this there was little agreement. Much of the difficulty derived from several secret treaties entered into by Britain and France during the war.[7] Sweeping concessions to Russia and Romania had been nullified, since both states had signed separate peace treaties with the enemy. As to Russia, however, the situation had not simplified. The publication by the Bolsheviks of the secret treaties they discovered upon their accession to power late in 1917 had the effect of portraying the Allies as cynically carving up subject peoples among themselves (while also heightening popular Italian territorial expectations). In Russia itself, a multi-faceted collection of civil and international wars wheezed indeterminately on. The Bolshevik government was under attack in both European Russia and Siberia by Russian forces of nearly every possible political persuasion, backed at times by various Allied powers. The situation was further complicated by anti-Soviet attacks, often with British or French blessing, by Polish, Finnish and Ukrainian forces and by the presence in several areas of military detachments and commissions from Britain, France, Japan and America. Beyond that, the sizeable Czech Legion was determinedly trying to fight its way out of Russia via Vladivostok, while assorted Allied powers and Russian groups tried equally determinedly to use it to their own varying ends. No Allied power had a clear-cut, consistent policy in the fluid Russian situation; much less was there any agreed Allied policy. Despite, or perhaps because of, the abrogation of the secret treaties, the entire Russian area, including its important European borderlands, remained a huge question mark. [8]

The other secret treaties remained in effect. They concerned the Middle East, the Balkans, and the Pacific area. These commitments had been made under the urgent wartime necessity of aid from Italy, Japan, the Arabs, and the Zionist movement. Some British radicals, liberals, and junior officials found these allocations of the spoils distasteful and, noting Wilson's view that America was not bound by these arrangements, hoped that he would somehow force Britain and France to abandon their treaty commitments. [9] This was expecting considerably more than Wilson could accomplish. Spurred by Chinese pleas and domestic political considerations, he did in the end strenuously oppose Japanese administrative and economic control of Shantung province in China but, faced by united opposition from Britain and France, tied to their treaty commitments, and with Japan in occupation, he had to give way. [10] Similarly, once Lloyd George had gained the German Pacific islands south of the Equator for Australia and New Zealand, he had no choice but to support Japan's undoubted treaty right to the German islands north of the Equator and defeat Wilson on that issue, too.

Wilson's efforts to modify the other secret treaties were more limited and no more successful. While he apparently had not been informed of the promises to Japan, Wilson had been told of the Middle Eastern and Italian arrangements upon American entry into the war, and perhaps this fact, coupled with his ignorance of the areas concerned and the absence of domestic pressure for revision, accounts for the half-heartedness of his attempts to upset the secret wartime arrangements.

The chief beneficiary of these arrangements was Italy, who in 1915 had been bribed by the secret Treaty of London into a declaration of war against the Central Powers by promise of massive amounts of Habsburg and Ottoman territory. Italy was to gain the Trentino, the South Tyrol, the Istrian peninsula, Trieste, portions of Dalmatia and Albania, and the Dodecanese Islands, plus some undefined rights to German colonies and to a share in the Ottoman Empire, particularly in Adalia in Anatolia. The entire Turkish situation was especially confused. With the collapse of the Russian commitments, there were no arrangements for European Turkey, but there was in 1917 a further concession of the Smyrna area in Anatolia to Italy and a series of conflicting commitments concerning the Arabic portions of the Ottoman Empire. The British had promised in 1915 that this territory, except perhaps Lebanon (a French interest), would become an Arab national state; had entered in 1916 into an Anglo-French division of the area between themselves; and had endorsed in 1917 the creation of a Jewish 'national home' in Palestine, which now was the subject of three conflicting arrangements. When in 1918 Wilson endorsed 'secure sovereignty' for the Turkish portions of the Ottoman Empire and 'autonomous development' for the remainder, the situation was in no way clarified.[11]

Allied oratory, while less binding than treaties, also muddied the situation and led to inflated expectations. In the hiatus before the peace conference, politicians in the victor countries raised in their battered, war-weary constituents unrealisable expectations of territorial aggrandisement, immediate prosperity, and a golden era of peace and happiness, as in Britain's 'land fit for heroes'. By war's end, the political leaders had committed themselves also to the growing movement for an international organisation to ensure lasting peace. From 1915 on, a variety of groups such as Britain's Fabian Society, Union of Democratic Control, and League of Nations Society, America's World Peace Foundation and League to Enforce Peace, and smaller movements on the continent earnestly planned for a new world order. Early in 1915 one of the Americans involved exulted: 'We have societies galore advocating a parliament of man and an equally large number of organizations and people advocating a supreme court of the world, all of them making innumerable suggestions and proposals at different times.'[12]

By war's end the concept of an international organisation was widely accepted in Britain and America and to a lesser degree on the continent, leading Wilson, Lloyd George, and some continental politicians to endorse the idea of a League of Nations, charged with the impossible task of preserving peace in perpetuity. Equally unrealisable were the implied promises by the politicians that the vanquished would assume the war costs of the victors, leaving them free to return to a prosperous pre-war life.

see
Seven
P. 78

Except with the Arabs, the victors were more cautious about commitments to subject nationalities, but repeated statements endorsing 'autonomy' came in time to be viewed by such peoples as support for independence. With the sudden collapse of the Central Powers the untiring efforts of the *émigré* groups had their reward. The Allies never really sanctioned the break-up of the Habsburg Empire.[13] It simply happened. In central Europe and on the Russian borderlands, as also briefly in the Middle East, new states seemed to emerge almost daily. Commitments or not, they were factors to be dealt with.

In the confused period before the peace conference opened, this complicated state of affairs was further compounded by an imperative need for haste. Winter was settling in, millions were starving (although not in Germany),* and influenza was sweeping the continent. It appeared that Soviet communism, new and equally feared as a fatal disease, might sweep westward as well. East of the Rhine, there existed a dangerous power vacuum as the four great eastern empires were in disarray. Despite much uncertainty, Germany retained some coherence, as did Turkey, but the vast Habsburg and Romanov domains were in complete collapse.[14] In this

---

* The persistent myth of deliberate Allied starvation of Germany is demonstrably untrue. The Germans were undernourished but not afflicted with the starvation conditions prevalent in many areas in the victor states. *FRUS PPC*, II 139–42, XII 115; P.R.O., F.O. 371/3776, *passim*. The related tale of the Allied blockade is equally mythical. True, under the armistice terms Allied warships remained in place to prevent a resumption of hostilities, but the Allies, who were short of merchant shipping and who had all Europe to feed, told the Germans to send out their ships to be filled with Allied food. This the Germans refused to do. In the end, Allied food was provided in Allied ships, the first deliveries arriving at the end of March 1919, well before German supplies were exhausted. Erich Eyck, *A History of the Weimar Republic* (Cambridge, Mass., 1962) I 88–9; Admiralty to F.O., 19 Apr 1919, m. 10630, F.O. 371/3776.

vacuum, the new states were emerging. Often they had no governments, and generally they had no boundaries, but they did seem to exist. Poland and Czechoslovakia were developing of their own accord. Bavaria was detaching itself from Germany; the Ukraine was resisting Russian control; and a short-lived republic of Kuban announced its existence. What eventually became the Baltic states were clamouring for independence, but nobody wanted to make decisions about that area until the outcome of the Russian civil wars became clear. In central and eastern Europe even the elementary problem of feeding people was rendered excruciatingly difficult by the fact that all administrative structure had been swept away by war and civil war, and none had yet been devised to replace it. There were, of course, less pressing problems affecting other parts of the globe, but parcelling out colonies and dividing up the German merchant fleet could wait. Europe could not. There the task was urgent.

Yet in the end Europe had to wait. When the plenipotentiaries finally convened at the French Foreign Ministry in the Quai d'Orsay in mid-January 1919, they did not deal with first things first. After the opening ceremonies, the urgent European tasks were avoided for some weeks. There were several reasons for this. Understandably, the Allied leaders wished to take each other's measure before they clashed head-on in the major battles, most of which were clearly going to come over European issues. The difficult question of Russian representation in the absence of any single Russian government, combined with deep-seated reluctance to recognise that of the Bolshevik Lenin while there remained any lingering hope of its defeat, led to a natural postponement of east European issues. As the great powers busied themselves with less-pressing non-European problems, Lloyd George, with dazzling diplomatic skill, secured most of Britain's desiderata and then hopped up to join Wilson on the pedestal where together they posed as the impartial arbiters of the world's destinies. In addition, since the five great states of Britain, France, America, Italy and Japan had arrogated all power of decision to themselves, leaving the twenty-two other countries officially present with little to do, these smaller states had to be given the appearance of some activity in order to placate their domestic opinion and prevent the fall of their governments. Accordingly, the two senior plenipotentiaries of each of the five great powers constituted themselves the

Council of Ten, before which the smaller states could plead and thus receive their day in the limelight. The smaller states made the most of this, reciting at interminable length documents already submitted and consuming weeks of valuable time. Another factor often considered to have increased the delay was Wilson's insistence on writing the Covenant of the League of Nations at the outset. He was probably correct in believing that it must be written first or not at all, and it is true that his League Commission met at night, thus not delaying the droning daytime sessions; but much of his energy and that of other senior officials was diverted for several weeks from the European issues which were becoming more urgent with each passing day.[15]

When the conference finally got down to business, it functioned very haphazardly. Much of the work was done by committees. Perhaps unfortunately, the various frontiers of Germany were assigned to several committees which functioned independently of each other. Most of these, in the belief that they were preparing bargaining documents for a subsequent peace congress with Germany, arrived at more stringent boundaries than might otherwise have been chosen. When the heads of the major delegations, minus Japan, tired of the Council of Ten, and constituted themselves the Big Four to meet at Wilson's home and settle matters, they proceeded in slipshod fashion without agenda, minutes, or any record of decisions until the secretary of the British delegation, the supremely efficient Colonel Sir Maurice Hankey, insinuated himself into their midst and rescued them from disaster.[16] Even then, the agenda darted from topic to topic, and the Big Four were startlingly erratic in either accepting, ignoring or rejecting expert reports, and in reserving a variety of questions, both major and minor, exclusively to themselves. For no ascertainable reason, the tangled but relatively trivial problem of Luxemburg was handled entirely by the Big Four without benefit of expert advice. In addition, while there was general agreement that the German treaty should be written first, the Italians, who were 'moral absentees'[17] on German issues and uninterested therein, demanded time for their particular concerns, thus forcing disastrous and heated forays by an ill-prepared Big Four into the morass of Balkan politics.

Influence and idiosyncracy, personality and prejudice all played their part in the haphazardness of decisions. While the legalistic

Lansing was officially the second American delegate, the entire conference recognised that only House had Wilson's ear and beat a path to his door. Similarly, in the French delegation André Tardieu, charged with guarding France's vital interests in western Europe, was the confidant of Premier Georges Clemenceau, and the others counted for nothing. In the British delegation, Lloyd George and the Foreign Secretary, Arthur James Balfour, mattered and perhaps Sir Eyre Crowe of the Foreign Office, but nobody else. The Italian Foreign Minister, Sidney Sonnino, was probably more influential than the Prime Minister, Vittorio Orlando, partly because he spoke English as well as French and partly because the British trusted him since his mother was Scottish. Wilson's inexperience in debate and penchant for involvement in trivia were factors, as were Lloyd George's refusal to read memoranda and reluctance to instruct his delegation. His secretary shielded him too well, and able British experts often worked at cross-purposes from lack of information. Much has been written about the charm of Eleutherios Venizelos of Greece and the prickly personality of Paul Hymans of Belgium, and these, too, played a part in the course of events.

The role of prejudice is perhaps best illustrated by the Polish question. Chiefly for strategic reasons, France wanted a powerful Poland. The Italians backed the French in supporting Polish claims in order to set a precedent for their own rather extravagant territorial demands elsewhere. Lloyd George, who was intensely anti-Polish in all respects, felt certain that Poland was going to be a dangerously unstable nuisance, so he fought to keep it as small as possible. On the other hand, the influential American expert on Poland, Robert Lord, was a historian recently converted to Roman Catholicism, who viewed Poland as a vital Christian outpost against the barbarian hordes to the east. When such prejudices were added to the inherent geographic, ethnic, and political difficulties of the problems, it is a wonder that any decisions were reached about Poland at all.

Yet somehow the decisions were made. They took so long that a certain realism intruded, and the idea of a subsequent congress with Germany was tacitly abandoned. Time pressures became so acute that the Versailles Treaty was, in the end, thrown together in a tremendous flurry and, despite the work of a territorial committee, never properly co-ordinated. When it was rushed to the printers while a German delegation patiently waited behind protective fencing at Versailles,[18] nobody had read it in full and nobody was very sure of its contents. None the less, this lengthy document of 440 clauses and over 200 pages was presented to the Germans in a tense ceremony at Versailles on 7 May 1919 essentially in the form of an ultimatum.

The Versailles Treaty,[19] which German representatives eventually had to sign on 28 June 1919 with little modification, was severe, but it is amazing that it was not more so. The interminable Allied battles throughout the spring over specific clauses amounted to a struggle between Anglo-American complacency, reinforced by the seas separating them from Germany, and French fear, reinforced by a long frontier with Germany.[20] In Wilson's mind there lingered some residue of the 'peace without victory' sentiment [21] and he was determined to see what he considered a just peace. The British wanted German ships and colonies but, in Europe, they still distrusted France, the ancient rival, and were already instinctively reverting to their traditional balance-of-power stance, designed to ensure that no power, including France, dominated the continent. Clemenceau, on the other hand, had seen two German invasions of France in his lifetime and knew well that France alone had not won this war. Like most Frenchmen, he craved security against what he saw as a continuing menace.

In the end it was two against one, and Clemenceau, appeased by the promise of an Anglo-American defensive guarantee which was never implemented, had to give way on many particulars. Thanks to Wilson's insistence that there be no dismemberment, Germany lost remarkably little territory, considering how thoroughly she had lost the war. True, the colonies were gone, but the European losses were relatively modest. In the south Germany lost nothing, and in the north only a small strip of Schleswig to neutral Denmark. In the west Germany was obliged to transfer two small districts, Eupen and Malmédy, to Belgium; to return Alsace-Lorraine to France, to the considerable displeasure of many of its inhabitants; and, as a consequence of one of the great battles among the Big Four, to cede the Saar coal-mines to France and the Saarland to the League of Nations for fifteen years, after which a plebiscite would determine the wishes of the population. The Rhineland was to be permanently demilitarised and temporarily occupied, but, to the distress of many Frenchmen, it remained German. To the east, the losses were greater. Memel went eventually to Lithuania, Danzig to the League of Nations as a Free City, and 122 square miles of upper Silesia to Czechoslovakia, while ultimately about one-third of upper Silesia went to Poland. Above all, the famous corridor, splitting East Prussia from the rest of Germany and consisting of portions of Posen and West Prussia, was ceded to Poland to give her access to the Baltic Sea. This was one of the most difficult decisions of the conference and one particularly resented by Germany, but it was probably the least bad solution to an impossible problem, particularly since a clear majority of the inhabitants of the Polish corridor were Polish, despite intensive German colonisation before the war.[22]

Germany, who shared Lloyd George's view of all things Polish, never accepted the 'bleeding border', but other clauses were equally offensive in German eyes. In an effort to ensure French security, the German military establishment was drastically reduced, Germany was largely disarmed, and the vaunted Prussian General Staff was to be disbanded (although, in fact, it soon reappeared under another name). In clauses which proved unrealisable Germany was obliged to surrender Kaiser Wilhelm II for trial by a special inter-Allied tribunal and other alleged war criminals on demand for trial in Allied military courts.* There were customs controls, restrictions on German economic policy, and an obligation to pay Allied occupation costs, which in the Rhineland were substantial. Above all, there were reparations.

The reparations clauses were among the least read, most written about, least understood, and most controversial sections of the Versailles Treaty. The basis for reparations arose from Wilson's Fourteen Points, which specified that occupied portions of France, Belgium, Romania, Serbia and Montenegro be 'restored'. During the armistice negotiations Germany was, on 6 November 1918, notified that this meant 'that compensation will be made by Germany for all the damage done to the civilian population of the Allies and their property by the aggression of Germany by land,

---

* The Kaiser had fled to neutral Holland and the Dutch declined to extradite him. The Allies compiled lists of many hundreds of other alleged war criminals but, in the end, only forty-five Germans, mostly very low-ranking, were charged for trial in a German civilian court at Leipzig. Twelve were actually brought to judgement, of whom the majority were acquitted. Erich Eyck, *A History of the Weimar Republic*, 2 vols (Cambridge, Mass., 1962) I 187–8.

by sea, and from the air'.[23] During the peace conference, there were repeated Allied efforts to stretch this statement to cover war costs, but Wilson was adamantly opposed to indemnities; therefore only Belgium, whose violation constituted a crime against international law as well as an act of aggression,* was accorded war costs.

The other Allies did succeed, however, in stretching reparation for damage done to cover such dubious items as war pensions and separation allowances, which appeared at the time to increase greatly the potential total figure.† The quarrel over reparations was so fraught with political implications that the Big Four eventually decided to make Germany theoretically responsible for all costs but actually responsible for a much narrower but somewhat expanded range of specific categories of largely civilian damages. As a result Article 231 of the Treaty, which was designed solely to provide the legal basis for reparations, read in full: 'The Allied and Associated Governments affirm, and Germany accepts, the responsibility of Germany and her Allies for causing all the loss and damage to which the Allied and Associated Governments and their nationals have been subjected as a consequence of a war imposed upon them by the aggression of Germany and her Allies.'

It is not widely known that, upon the principle of collective responsibility, the same clause, *mutatis mutandis*, was incorporated in the Treaty of Saint-Germain-en-Laye with Austria (Article 177) and the Treaty of Trianon with Hungary (Article 161); that there is no explicit mention of 'war guilt'; that this clause appears only in the reparations section of the treaty; and that, by Article 232, Germany's financial responsibility was restricted to civilian damages, as somewhat loosely defined in an annex. In later years Germany, secure in the realisation that few people would engage in the requisite analysis of three treaties, was able to fulminate to great effect about the patent injustice of 'unilateral war guilt'.

The other difficulty with the reparations clauses was that the

---

* Under the 1839 treaties, Germany pledged to defend the independence, territorial integrity, and compulsory neutrality of Belgium. In the first week of the war, Chancellor Theobald von Bethmann-Hollweg acknowledged Germany's guilt respecting Belgium before the Reichstag and promised full restitution.[24]

† As the German reparations debt was ultimately established in 1921 on the basis of an assessment of German capacity to pay, inclusion of pensions and allowances affected only the distribution of receipts, not the total liability.

total figure for German liability was not set. This stemmed partly
from Wilson's determination to verify the damages claimed and
partly from the awkward political fact that public opinion in most
receiver states anticipated amounts far in excess of German capacity
to pay. Thus, inclusion of any realistic figure would have caused
the fall of several governments. It was to Germany's advantage that
the reparations debt be left unsettled, for figures discussed at the
conference were astronomic, ranging as high as sixteen times the
amount eventually set in 1921, but the absence of a set sum also
gave Germany the propaganda advantage of being able to com-
plain about signing a 'blank cheque'.

The capstone of the Versailles Treaty was the Covenant of the
League of Nations. The peace settlement forwarded international
law in several ways, notably through the Labour Charter and
clauses pertaining to international waterways, but the western
world's imagination and Wilson's hopes centred on the Covenant
of the League of Nations, which he unwisely insisted upon incor-
porating in all of the treaties on the assumption that such would
ensure approval by the American Senate. Equally unwisely, Wilson
accepted other treaty clauses which he considered unjust in the
expectation that the League could later remedy such defects. However, the Covenant clause requiring unanimity in all actions of
consequence rendered the League an instrument of the *status quo*
and severely restricted its ability to engage in any significant
activity at all. The Covenant provided for an Assembly of all
member nations, a Council dominated by the great powers, a
Secretariat at Geneva, a Permanent Court of International Justice
later established at The Hague, and some rather ill-defined
measures to be taken against disturbers of the peace. Despite
intense Japanese efforts, the Anglo-Saxon powers would not
tolerate any clause, however ambiguous, in support of racial
equality. The resultant organisation did its best work in consoli-
dating the specialised agencies, many of them pre-existing, and to
a lesser degree, in alleviating somewhat the lot of the inhabitants
of former colonies of the defeated powers. None the less, in its
larger role the League foundered on the twin rocks of the unanimity
clause and the absence of America. Beyond that the League lacked
any substantial enforcement powers, any answer to the fundamental
impracticality of collective security, or any solution to the inevitable
conflict between a supra-national organisation and the claims of

national sovereignty, which had only been rendered more strident by the war and the peace.[25] In the circumstances the League was foredoomed to failure, and its creation constituted one of the dangerously misleading illusions of the peace.

The Versailles Treaty has been sharply criticised and some of the criticisms are valid although, given the circumstances in which it was hastily patched together, it is remarkable that it was not much more unsatisfactory. It has often been said, and with reason, that the Treaty was too much of a compromise between thoroughly opposed positions, too soft to restrain Germany and yet too severe to be acceptable to most Germans.[26] Either a fully Wilsonian treaty or a fully French treaty might have been better, although even a fully Wilsonian treaty would have been unacceptable to Germany as it would have involved some territorial loss to Poland. In any event the awkward accommodation of Wilsonian idealism and French cynicism soon proved unworkable, and a powerful, resentful Germany, determined to break the bonds of the Versailles *diktat*, disturbed the tranquillity of Europe throughout the interwar years. Since the Versailles Treaty together with the east European settlement left this powerful, resentful Germany surrounded by smaller, weaker states, most of whose populations contained substantial German minorities, the potential for future discord was obvious to Germany's fearful neighbours. On the whole the peacemakers at Paris did not recognise the danger inherent in a situation where Germany was no longer surrounded and checked by great empires. They assumed erroneously that Germany would abide by their decisions and accept her new neighbours.

The Versailles Treaty was also criticised for lack of attention to economic realities,[27] but in fact enormous care had been taken to preserve economic units at the expense of ethnic coherence. It was an economic reality supported by an ethnic majority which led to the creation of the Polish corridor. Similarly, the retention of German-speaking Egerland by a reluctant Czechoslovakia was dictated by economic and strategic considerations. A more serious problem was that such enforcement provisions as there were depended entirely upon continuing harmony of viewpoint among the victors. To the extent that it ever existed, this harmony evaporated immediately and, as a consequence, much of the Treaty fell by the wayside. It could be argued that, aside from the territorial clauses and the complex created in the German mind, the peace of Versailles was of relatively little importance because so little of it was enforced.

The real difficulty was not that the Treaty was exceptionally unfair but that the Germans thought it was, and in time persuaded others that it was. Germany complained that the Treaty violated the Fourteen Points, but reserved her sharpest complaints, as with regard to Poland, for clauses most securely anchored on the Fourteen Points (to the extent that Wilson's wartime slogans could be fulfilled with any precision at all). German territorial losses were perhaps greater than they might have been if the Big Four had had time to consider the matter as a whole, but the Versailles Treaty was not exceptionally harsh, considering how thoroughly Germany had lost a long and bitter war. However, the German people, whose territory had not been invaded and whose war damage was non-existent, rapidly convinced themselves that they had not lost the war. If they had not lost the war, *any* diminution of territory and any restriction was by definition unfair. The German people expected without reason that Wilson would ensure them a 'just peace', which in their eyes meant Germany's 1914 frontiers and no penalties at all. Despite the widespread shock when the terms became known, there is clear evidence that the German people and government began reacting intensely to the Versailles Treaty before it was written, and that they were in fact reacting to a defeat which they would not acknowledge.[28] The real difficulty with the Versailles Treaty was that, for the moment, it represented reality. Since this reality was of short duration, so also was the Treaty.

When the Versailles Treaty was duly signed on 28 June 1919 with appropriate ceremonial, the leading statesmen departed, leaving completion of the other treaties to lesser lights. Much work had already been done on the settlement with the other central powers, particularly in matters of interest to Italy. As a consequence it was clear that there would be many territorial changes and several new states, but much work remained. It was done piecemeal from July 1919 to August 1920 by a series of steadily less eminent Allied representatives.

The job of writing four more major treaties was simplified by the fact that much material could be carried over from the Treaty of Versailles. The treaties with Austria, Hungary, Bulgaria and Turkey,[29] all signed in Paris suburbs, each incorporated the *dfn : + movement of German Plant to S.U.*

League Covenant and the Labour Charter. They all called for the surrender of alleged war criminals and contained disarmament clauses which differed from the German model only in detail, in the size of the armies permitted, and in that such restrictions were more enforceable against small states than against a major power. Each treaty contained financial and economic clauses and customs restrictions similar to those of the Versailles settlement and, while the geographic particulars inevitably varied, the principles of the German model regarding ports, international waterways, and rail transit were carried over. Each treaty contained reparations clauses which, despite considerable variance in detail, owed much to the reparations section of the Versailles Treaty, although in fact Austria was so impoverished that she paid no reparations except credits for the transfer of state properties. All of the Central Powers were obliged to assume occupation and commission costs as a prior charge on their payments. Beyond this the four treaties, unlike the German settlement, acknowledged the transformation of Serbia into the Kingdom of the Serbs, Croats and Slovenes (hereafter called Yugoslavia although this name did not become official until 1929) and contained a series of clauses designed to protect the rights of ethnic minorities within their territories. All the small states of eastern Europe were soon required to undertake similar obligations toward minorities. To their indignation, the great powers were not afflicted with such restrictions.

The eastern treaties, combined with the ultimate settlements along the Russian borderlands, created a string of new or greatly enlarged states from Finland on the Baltic to Yugoslavia on the Adriatic. In part these decisions derived from intense nationalistic pressures and from an effort to redraw the map of Europe along ethnic lines. Beyond that, France, for obvious strategic reasons, supported the creation of sizeable states on Germany's eastern and southern borders. Another important factor was fear of communism.[30] Thus, the Baltic states were finally allowed to be when the Soviet triumph became evident, and Romania, abysmally defeated in the war, emerged roughly doubled in size. While ethnic considerations played a part, the string of successor states known as the *cordon sanitaire* was also designed as a bulwark against the revolutionary virus. In the north these territorial decisions awaited the outcome of the Russian civil wars and were not incorporated in the Paris settlement, but the territorial changes in central Europe were made at the expense of the defunct Habsburg Empire and were delimited in the treaties with its heirs.

The Austrian and Hungarian treaties followed the German model particularly closely and were very similar. Indeed it was originally planned to present the two treaties simultaneously to the twin heirs of the Habsburg Empire, but the advent of Bela Kun's communist regime in Hungary caused a delay until Hungary had a government which the great powers were willing to recognise. As a result the Treaty of Saint-Germain-en-Laye with Austria was signed on 10 September 1919, while the Treaty of Trianon was held in abeyance until 4 June 1920. Both states were obligated to preserve their independence and to abstain from any act compromising it. Austrian *Anschluss* (union) with Germany was forbidden, although both Germanic states desired it, for the peacemakers realised that if Germany sat astride the Danube, its dominance of south-eastern Europe would be complete. Austria and Hungary each renounced the Habsburg monarchy and all Habsburg rights, privileges, and properties overseas. Both treaties contained reparations sections virtually identical with that of the Versailles Treaty. And both states suffered exceptionally severe and damaging territorial losses.

The truncation of Austria was particularly catastrophic. To Italy went the Istrian peninsula, the Trentino, and the predominantly Germanic south Tyrol. The Treaty of Saint-Germain also created the state of Czechoslovakia, the Czech portions of which comprised the most productive of the former Austrian domains. Galicia went to Poland and Bukovina to Romania, while Yugoslavia gained Bosnia–Herzegovina, the Dalmatian coast, and a number of coastal islands. What remained to Austria was a landlocked little mountain state with nearly a third of its population concentrated in Vienna and the rest scattered around an unproductive Alpine hinterland. The capital of a vast empire remained, but the empire to support it was gone. Interwar Austria was to prove an economic impossibility. Indeed acute deficit financing and colossal inflation led to bankruptcy in 1922. After financial reconstruction under League auspices, the Austrian economy limped through the twenties on the crutch of foreign loans.[31]

Hungarian territorial losses were even more severe but left a more economic, if also more irredentist, state. Hungary was obliged to cede much of the Burgenland to Austria, while both

Slovakia and Ruthenia went to Czechoslovakia. Yugoslavia took Croatia–Slavonia and part of the Banat. The rest of the Banat, along with Transylvania and part of the Hungarian plain, went to Romania. The one remaining outlet to the sea, Fiume, was also surrendered, although its disposition was still unsettled despite a tense battle at Paris between Wilson and the Italians. While acute postwar economic and political dislocation led to financial crisis and financial reconstruction by the League in 1924, the surviving remnant of Hungary was none the less economically viable, thanks to its fertile plains. However, three million Magyars were left outside the contracted frontiers,[32] a fact which Hungary neither forgave nor forgot.

Bulgaria was luckier. Its territorial losses were relatively modest. Under the Treaty of Neuilly of 27 November 1919, Yugoslavia received several small strategic border salients, Romania regained the southern Dobruja, and Greece took western Thrace, thus blocking Bulgarian access to the Aegean Sea and the Mediterranean, but that was all. Bulgaria was also fortunate in that her reparations debt was specifically limited to $2\frac{1}{4}$ milliard gold francs (£90 millions or $450 millions) payable in semi-annual instalments over thirty-seven years.

Of all the eastern treaties, that with Turkey was the most complicated, the last signed, and the shortest lived.[33] Under the Treaty NB of Sèvres of 10 August 1920 the straits from the Black Sea to the Mediterranean were opened in peace and war to the merchant and war ships of all nations, and control of the straits was vested in an international commission. The pre-war capitulatory regime of extraterritorial rights for westerners was preserved and extended to those Allies which had not previously participated in it. In view of the severity of Turkey's territorial losses, reparations were waived except for narrowly defined civilian damages, to the extent that funds were available after service of the pre-war Ottoman debt and payment of the inevitable occupation and commission costs.

Turkish territorial losses were indeed severe although Ottoman pre-war control of some areas had been ephemeral, and several clauses of the treaty merely confirmed pre-existing situations. Thus Turkey renounced all rights in the Sudan and Libya and recognised the French protectorates in Morocco and Tunis, the British protectorate in Egypt, and the British annexation of Cyprus. In the Middle East the Hedjaz (now Saudi Arabia) was to become an independent kingdom, while Syria, Mesopotamia, and Palestine were to become mandates under major power control. Mandate was the new term applied to former German and Turkish colonies transferred to the victors under nominal League supervision. For the Middle East, the mandatory powers were not enumerated in the Treaty of Sèvres but in fact had been decided at the San Remo conference in April 1920. France took Syria and Lebanon, while Britain gained the rest, namely Palestine, Transjordan and Iraq.[34] Finally, in a British and Zionist triumph, the Balfour Declaration of 2 November 1917, endorsing 'a national home' for the Jews in Palestine, was imposed there as an obligation upon the mandatory power (Britain), notwithstanding prior pledges first to the Arabs and then to the French, and expert advice to the contrary.[35]

In partial fulfilment of the Treaty of London, Turkey ceded a number of Aegean islands to Italy. In a decision related both to the tangled history of the Treaty of London and to the Fiume quarrel, the Smyrna (Izmir) district in Anatolia went to Greece.[36] As a result of a dubious Anglo-American manoeuvre in response to Italian insistence on Fiume, to which Italy was not entitled under the London Treaty, Greece was already in possession of Smyrna. Turkey retained sovereignty over the area, but the exercise of this sovereignty was to be transferred to Greece for five years, after which the local parliament could petition the League Council for incorporation into Greece, with a plebiscite to be at the discretion of the Council. Greece also received some of Turkey's Aegean islands and, from European Turkey, the substantial territory of eastern Thrace. Beyond all that, Kurdistan was to become either autonomous or independent, according to the preference of its inhabitants, and Armenia was to become an independent state with boundaries to be set by Wilson (but, in the end, Armenia was absorbed by Soviet Russia in 1920 and Turkey retained Kurdistan).

The Treaty of Sèvres was never ratified. Even before its terms were completed Sultan Mohammed VI's subservience to the Allies coupled with the Greek landing at Smyrna generated a nationalist revolt under the leadership of Mustapha Kemal. His success, particularly against French troops, led to a British occupation of Istanbul in March 1920, thus rendering the Sultan a virtual prisoner. In response the national movement swelled, and in April created a new National Assembly in Ankara. There ensued a two-year Greco-Turkish war, expulsion of the Greeks from Anatolia, the fall of the Sultan and the eventual proclamation of a republic under Kemal, and, in the last stages of the war, a dangerous Anglo-Turkish military confrontation in the autumn of 1922. As a consequence, after protracted negotiation, the Treaty of Lausanne, to replace that of Sèvres, was signed on 24 July 1923.[37] By its terms Turkey regained Smyrna, eastern Thrace, and some of the Aegean islands. She was also relieved of all capitulations, reparations, and military limitations except the demilitarised zone of the straits. A Greco-Turkish convention provided for a forced population exchange which proved ruthless in its execution, but which at least eliminated the minorities problems which plagued central and eastern Europe.

The creation of an unending series of minority problems is only one of many grounds upon which the Paris peace settlement as a whole has been sharply criticised. There were indeed large minorities all over eastern Europe as frontiers based on ethnic lines proved impossible of realisation, especially in areas of mixed nationalities. Estimates of minority populations vary widely, and official censuses are unreliable because governments tried to minimise minority totals, but even the roughest statistics indicate the immensity of the problem. Poland, a country of 27 millions, contained 18 million Poles by Polish count, but far fewer by other estimates. There were also at least a million Germans, 3 to 5 million Ukrainians, a million White Russians, and 2 or 3 million Jews, the vast majority of them culturally distinct. Czechoslovakia's total population of 14¼ millions included 3¼ million Germans, three-quarters of a million Magyars, and half a million Ruthenes. Romania's 18 millions contained at least three-quarters of a million Germans, 1½ to 2 million Magyars, half a million Ukrainians, 360,000 Bulgarians, and perhaps a quarter of a million Russians. The surviving remnant of Hungary, despite her drastic truncation, still contained, in a total population of 18 millions, about half a million Germans, half a million Ukrainians, half a million Jews, and a quarter of a million Slovaks. Yugoslavia's 12 millions included, in addition to her three major native ethnic components, half a million Germans, half a million Magyars, half a million Albanians, and a quarter of a million Romanians. There were also about 600,000 Macedonians whom Yugoslavia counted as Serbs, although Bulgaria, with some reason, insisted that they were Bulgars. While these startling east-European minorities could undoubtedly have been reduced somewhat by different boundaries, generally at the expense of economic considerations, it is self-evident that nothing short of massive population transfers could have resolved the problem.

A contradictory complaint about the Paris peace settlement has been that economic factors were ignored in favour of ethnic considerations. On the contrary it was the effort to reconcile ethnic groupings with economic and strategic necessities which led to the creation of so many minorities. The peacemakers acknowledged that when the language line crossed a vital railway five times in twenty-six miles, ethnicity had to yield to economics. The difficulty of drawing boundaries was further compounded by the cagey east-European peasant's refusal to commit himself lest he later find himself on the wrong side of the frontier and part of a persecuted minority. Thus enquiries into ethnic allegiance often evoked the reply, 'I am an inhabitant of this place.'

One of the more common criticisms of the settlement, apart from those made by interested parties such as the Italians, Hungarians, Chinese and Arabs, was the argument that the Allies should have restored the Austro-Hungarian Empire, which was an excellent economic unit, if not a successful political entity.[38] While the central European settlement had economic disadvantages, particularly for Austria itself, it seems evident that the Habsburg Empire had dissolved of its own volition and could not have been restored without sustained use of force. More valid perhaps is the argument that Wilson's insistence on self-determination for all nationalities led to the fragmentation of Europe into too many small states, some of them neither democratic nor economic nor by any standard very satisfactory.[39] The peacemakers did recognise that the disintegration of the Habsburg Empire and the fragmentation of eastern Europe would generate economic problems when raw materials fell on one side of a new boundary and processing plants on the other. Indeed sometimes a given manufacturing process of the old Habsburg Empire was now spread among as many as three new states. To alleviate this problem the peace treaties had provided for a substantial measure of economic integration among the succession states. But intense political nationalism inevitably engendered an economic nationalism which rendered economic co-operation impossible.

While the east-European settlement certainly created new

difficulties, an acute observer and student of the interwar European scene has remarked that probably more people were reasonably satisfied with their governments then than at any time before or since,[40] and this comment cannot be disregarded. It has been argued that the fragmentation of Europe fanned a dangerous nationalism, and certainly the history of interwar Poland's squabbles with most of her neighbours tends to confirm the thesis. Yet one must consider whether the nationalist pressures which had been building for a century could possibly have been denied in the aftermath of Armageddon and whether the dangers were not perhaps more apparent than actual, since small states can rarely launch large wars. When one contemplates the conflicting claims of ethnicity and economics, one must conclude that the most balanced judgement was that of King Albert of the Belgians: 'What would you have? They did what they could.'[41]

There were, however, serious inadequacies in the settlement, some of which could not have been avoided except perhaps by greater injustice. One of the difficulties was that, while so much had been done, so much remained undone. So many questions remained unresolved. Perhaps fortunately, none of the reparations debts except that of Bulgaria had been established, but the ensuing uncertainty further strained war-battered economies in defeated and victor states alike. Nor were the boundaries definitively set. All over Europe boundary commissions went forth, some of them armed with considerable latitude, to delimit the borders with precision. Some of their difficulties dragged on for years, and one part of the Belgo-German frontier was not settled until 1931. Furthermore, from Schleswig to Kurdistan, there were a series of plebiscite zones where the inhabitants were to determine their own future. With the exception of the Saar, these decisions were completed by the end of 1921, but there had been two years of uncertainty in the interim. The fate of Fiume had not been determined.* Nothing involving Russia had been settled. When the Paris con-

---

* The Fiume settlement was protracted. In September 1919 freebooters under the Italian poet Gabriele d'Annunzio occupied the city. In November 1920, by the Treaty of Rapallo, Italy and Yugoslavia agreed that Fiume would become a Free City, and Italian forces expelled d'Annunzio. However, the Italian troops remained, finally taking full control in September 1923. In January 1924, by the Treaty of Rome, the Yugoslavs recognised the *fait accompli* and the award of the city to Italy, while the remainder of the Free State went to Yugoslavia.

ference ended Finland had become a state, but its Karelian borderlands with Russia were still a battleground; the Baltic states still
did not know whether they were to be; and Poland did not have
an eastern boundary. Only in October 1920 was the Finnish frontier defined; only in 1921 and 1922 were the Baltic republics of
Lithuania, Latvia and Estonia formally recognised; and only after
a Russo-Polish war with substantial French involvement was the
Russo-Polish frontier set in the Treaty of Riga of 18 March 1921.[42]
In remarking that the peacemakers at Paris did what they could,
one must also remember how much they could not do.

Another difficulty with the settlement was that it was based on
assumptions which proved unsound. One such assumption was
that all states would approve the treaties. Not only Turkey refused
but also China, enraged by the Shantung decision. Germany and
Hungary were only brought to ratification by extreme pressure, a
circumstance which rendered the binding effect of the settlement
questionable. Furthermore by the time the first treaty, that of
Versailles, took effect on 10 January 1920, American approval of
the settlement appeared doubtful. The peace structure was based
upon the premise of full American participation, and the erratic
American withdrawal over a period of four years caused first great
uncertainty and then acute dislocation of the entire settlement.*
The settlement was further dislocated by disagreement among the
remaining victors. The elaborate peace structure, which contained
remarkably little provision for enforcement, was predicated upon
continuing and increased identity of Allied viewpoint but, as
America withdrew, as Italy pursued her own concerns and showed
little interest in much else, as Britain and France quarrelled about
everything from submarines to Silesia, from Turkey to Tangier,
from reparations to Russia to the Rhineland, decisions became
increasingly difficult to reach and tended to ineffectual compromises.

* The American Senate twice rejected the Versailles Treaty: on 19 Novem-
ber 1919 and 19 March 1920. Therefore the United States never joined the
League of Nations. In August 1921 America signed separate treaties with
Germany, Austria and Hungary, which confirmed her in her privileges but not
in her responsibilities under the treaties of Versailles, Saint-Germain, and
Trianon. Senate approval was contingent upon the reservation that the United
States would not participate in any treaty commissions without Congressional
consent. This to all practical effect ended American participation in the peace
structure, although American troops remained in the Rhineland until January
1923.

The peacemakers had not only assumed that they could agree upon the implementation of their treaties. They had also assumed that the affected peoples would abide by their decisions. Yet several nations, including Poland, Turkey, Hungary and, above all, Germany, would not. During 1920 the peacemakers completed their peace treaties, and the elaborate optimistic structure of commissions to carry them out came into being. Yet the French at least were painfully aware that winning the peace would prove as arduous as winning the war. The battle was joined without delay.

2 The Effort to Enforce the Peace

ALTHOUGH the Paris peace settlement dealt with the entire globe, it was a peculiarly European peace, written largely by the European victors to their own benefit. Despite nominal Japanese participation and Wilson's efforts toward a new world order, the treaties reflected Europe's view of the world and of its own role in it. Most of the assumptions upon which European leaders operated had, however, been rendered obsolete by the First World War. In this sense the settlement was anachronistic.

Since the west-European states emerged victorious in the struggle with Germany, thanks in part to the contributions of Russia, America and Japan, they did not recognise that they had lost their pre-eminence and their position as rulers of the world. Civil war in Russia and China, together with isolationism and economic self-absorption in America, obscured the extent of the shift in the power balance, as did the distribution of additional colonies to Britain and France. The assumption that it was Europe's absolute right to rule the world clouded the picture even further and helped Europeans of all classes to overlook hard economic realities.

Before the war Europe had (along with America) taken over the globe, easily subjecting the non-white races, thanks to a wide technological gap, ample capital, military superiority, and division among native peoples. In justification of its rule Europe cited its 'white man's burden' to civilise, Christianise, and modernise. The peace settlement continued this process as the colonies of the foe were distributed among the victors. True, Japan had to be conceded the north Pacific islands as she was already in occupation, but this unhappy fact could be mitigated by the thought that Japan was much the most westernised Asian nation, the occidental of the Orient. For the rest the sun still never set on a much-enlarged British Empire, nor for that matter on an enlarged French Empire. London remained the great pulsing heart of 'the Empire' and Paris of 'France indivisible'. Imperialism appeared triumphant, despite the faint disguise of mandates. In fact it was on the wane, and the spotlight was starting to move away from Europe as power dispersed, particularly to America and Asia.

Europeans, especially western Europeans, did not recognise this fact. Large or small, European states shared a common but outdated world view. Most Europeans assumed that Europe was the centre of the world, of civilisation, and of culture. What happened in Europe was what mattered. Tension between France and Italy seemed far more significant than tension between Japan and China, although which nations were on the rise and which on the wane was no secret to the far-sighted. Except for Europe's offspring, America (whose sheer power in several senses, especially financial, commanded attention on the rare occasions when she insisted) and the 'white dominions', the rest of the world consisted of 'wogs' to be economically exploited for European profit and to be gradually – very gradually – civilised into imitation of European systems of government, law, religion, industry and culture. While eschewing additional colonies Americans expressed similar attitudes in more forthright language. A midwestern senator once exulted, 'With God's help, we will lift Shanghai up and up, ever up, until it is just like Kansas City.'[1]

The bases of western rule had been primarily economic, technological and psychological. One of the most potent and least costly weapons had been the absolute conviction of inherent superiority. The European club had divisions within itself but its members stood above all others. Lord Curzon, the pre-war British Viceroy in India and postwar Foreign Secretary, once remarked that Frenchmen 'are not the sort of people one would go tiger-shooting with'.[2] If necessary, however, Curzon would have found it possible to go tiger-shooting with a Frenchman or an American or perhaps a Czech, but not with an Indian princeling, even one holding a better degree from Oxford than his own. Indians, along with other Asians and Africans, were *Untermenschen* (subhumans), regarded by Englishmen in essentially the same light that Nazi Germans later viewed Slavic peoples.

When Curzon ruled India, 4000 Britons could easily hold that vast, teeming subcontinent in thraldom and in security against all comers. No longer. Inherent white superiority was increasingly challenged by subject peoples, while nascent nationalism made the old policy of divide and conquer decreasingly effective. The cost of maintaining European domination had sharply escalated while European resources available for this task were on the decline, largely as a result of the war. Debt-ridden European governments could not afford vastly increased military expenditures to compensate for the evaporation of inherent superiority. Beyond that, moral debts were falling due for the substantial African and Asian contribution to the carnage of Flanders fields. In the circumstances, European overlords made concessions as slowly as possible to peoples who seemed not quite real and who clearly did not matter, while themselves intending to hold as much as possible as long as possible. The implications of their own attitude escaped most Europeans.

The political balance was also shifted by economic change. Imperialism, technology, and changing tastes had created an interlocking world economy. America was more self-sufficient than any other highly developed nation but, even so, as canned vegetables, automobiles, and Coca-Cola became commonplace, her imports of African kola nuts along with Asian tin and rubber soared. Despite the most balanced of major European economies, France also lacked tin and rubber, along with oil and several minerals vital to modern technology. Britain, Italy and Japan were all heavily dependent on imported raw materials and food as well. All traded fairly heavily with America, which added to the pattern of interdependence, as did the fact that the industrial powers were dependent on each other's colonies for basic resources. Colonies, of course, existed to be exploited to the benefit of Europe but, as subject peoples increasingly rejected this assumption, the threat to Europe's long-term future grew.

The economic balance itself had also shifted sharply as a direct consequence of the war. Europe had squandered her treasure, in money as well as in blood. As all the European victors were deeply in debt to America, the world's financial capital had moved from the City of London to Wall Street. During the war, as Britain concentrated her energies upon survival, her lucrative carrying trade on the world's oceans was pre-empted by America, while her traditional Asian and Latin-American markets were taken over by Japan and the United States. After more than four years of total war, economic as well as military, European industry was either utterly ravaged, as in Belgium and northern France, or utterly exhausted, as in Britain where production had been maximal and maintenance minimal. Moreover, since western Europe had been industrialised before the rest of the world, it now had the oldest and most inefficient mines and factories, which could no longer compete with new, modern facilities elsewhere. Much of western Europe's industrial structure was obsolete.

The economic organisation of Europe was equally obsolete. An old Spanish saying declares, 'Wide is Castile'.[3] So it was in the fifteenth century and so also was Spain in the sixteenth century. But by the early nineteenth century, Spain was merely an impoverished little appendage to a Europe dominated by five great and glittering powers. Now, after an orgy of destruction multiplied by modern technology, the glitter was gone and there remained an impoverished small continent cut up into some thirty competing little states. As inadequate domestic markets could not consume the yield of mass production and tariff barriers inhibited exports, businessmen soon saw the need for a larger economic unit and began to advocate various forms of European economic union, chiefly in hopes of more effective competition with America. But most political leaders and ordinary Europeans paid them little heed, focusing instead on the traditional European national rivalries. After all, that was what mattered.

The obsolete European assumption that Europe constituted the civilised world and that Europe's quarrels were what counted could be found all across the continent. This view of most of the rest of the world as inferior and unimportant (except in respect to the strategic position and economic power of European states) transcended centuries-old European rivalries and hatreds. While Franco-German tension was not necessarily the single most serious problem of the interwar world, all Europe thought it was. Certainly it completely eclipsed events in Palestine, where tiresome natives seemed to misbehave so often. Almost without exception the European imperial states, large or small, assumed that it was their mission to rule the world in accordance with their interests and to bring it into conformity with their values, while the European non-imperial states assumed that Europe *was* the world.

This outdated European view was clearly reflected in the organisation created to preserve the new world order. In most respects the League of Nations was a European club, dominated by European statesmen, European assumptions, and European issues most of the time. Throughout the history of the League Japan was the only non-European state ever to hold a permanent seat on the Council, and in the early years Europe monopolised most of the non-permanent seats as well. Of the 63 states belonging to the League at one time or another, 29 (including Turkey) were European. A Latin-American bloc of 20 states was entitled to no permanent seat and one non-permanent seat on the Council. There were 6 Asian members of the League (3 Near-Eastern and 3 Far-Eastern) and 3 from Africa, representing *all* the independent or quasi-independent nations of those two continents in the interwar period. Finally, the British Empire held 5 seats occupied by India and the white dominions (including South Africa, where indeed only the white minority was represented, often by an Englishman).

Without exception the prominent figures in the halls of the League at Geneva were European. The great powers dominated, but the most conspicuous devotees of the League were the representatives of the smaller European states, especially those which had been beneficiaries of the peace settlement. These states, frightened of Russia or Germany or both, tended to cling to the League and to the illusion that it could protect them and their gains. They were the leading champions of collective security, secure in the knowledge that their smallness ensured that they would never be called upon to provide it. Generally they viewed the world as bounded by the Urals and the Azores, unless they were imperial overlords themselves, as were Belgium, Denmark, Holland and Portugal.

The great powers were less enthusiastic. If collective security ever materialised they would be expected to ensure it, and no state was eager to accept such an unlimited, universal military commitment. Since they were among the strong nations of the world the European great powers were not attracted to a system intended to protect the weak against the strong. This new system was rendered palatable, however, by the fact that it enshrined the old order, giving the haves a privileged position *vis-à-vis* the have-nots, and bestowing moral sanction on all aspects, cultural, economic and political, of the existing Darwinian imperial structure of European domination. To a considerable degree the League system disguised the transfers of power taking place in the world and reinforced Europe's view of its role.

After centuries of experience in statecraft and great power politics Europe had developed a certain cynicism which led its leaders to recognise that many of the premises upon which the

League rested were naive. The theory of collective security assumed an astonishing amount of agreement and altruism among men and nations, an unfailing willingness to sacrifice and die for strangers. The structure of the new world organisation also assumed, despite the historical record, that men and nations naturally and consistently would prefer conciliation and peace to competition and war. Should a nation deviate from such beatific behaviour, world opinion would deter its transgressions. This extraordinary assumption rested in turn upon four others: that world opinion necessarily existed at all on a given issue, that it was united, that it was unfailingly on the side of the angels, and that it would provide an effective counter to force. Their wartime experience told Europe's leaders that guns were more reliable.

Yet guns and gunboats now cost more than European powers could afford. Besides, the old Concert of the great powers was in disrepute, along with the traditional balance-of-power mechanism. In its place was the League of Nations, supposedly a new order, but in fact, even officially, one preserving the special position of the great powers. Europe's leaders quickly recognised that the decisions would continue to be made in Berlin, London, Paris and Rome or by consultation among their representatives. That being so, they consented to contribute to the oratory of Geneva and to pay lip service to its tenets, although always with extreme caution concerning collective security.

The leaders of the European great powers also recognised what ordinary men often did not: that the League was a limited agency of limited functions and effect. It was an agency of persuasion and conciliation and little more. Since its Covenant did not ban the use of force and the League itself had no force of its own, it could not ensure any nation's security, particularly when threatened by a major power. There was no real prospect that the League could fulfil its chief function of enforcing and preserving the peace. That could only be done by the great powers, provided that they were either in agreement or in precarious balance.

As the new League turned in 1920 to its assigned task of enforcing and preserving the peace, it discovered that the great powers had largely reserved enforcement to themselves or their agencies and that, in many areas, before peace could be preserved, it must first be established. To the dismay of many, peace did not obligingly 'break out' when it was officially declared. Indeed during the peace

conference, General Sir Henry Wilson, Chief of the Imperial
General Staff, remarked that twenty-one wars were then in progress, and in March 1920 he wrote, 'This Peace Treaty has resulted
in war everywhere.'[4] While exaggerated, his judgement was essentially sound. The advent of peace was highly relative. The major
powers were no longer in bloody collision, but civil war raged in
Russia, Ireland, China, Turkey, and briefly in the Ruhr. Foreign
troops remained in Russia; the Baltic area was a battleground; and
Poland invaded Russia while Hungary marched briefly on Poland,
Romania, and Slovakia.[5] There was fighting on the Finnish
frontier and in Fiume; in Silesia Germans and Poles waged an
undeclared war; most Balkan borders were aflame; and in Anatolia
the Turks fought the Greeks, backed by the British. Yet the world
was officially at peace.

In time the little wars fizzled out. In 1922 the last Japanese
troops left Siberia, and Lenin was in firm control of a Marxist
government which no major power yet recognised. By then the Red
Army had marched on Warsaw, France had rushed to Poland's
rescue, and after much difficulty, Russia's western frontiers had
finally been set.[6] In 1921 the last Polish–German boundaries,
including that in Silesia, were settled by plebiscite, and the creation
of the Irish Free State ended the fighting in Ireland. Late in 1922
an armistice silenced the guns in Turkey. By that time the world
had learned that peace treaties are easier to write than to implement.

The peace treaties provided for numerous commissions to execute
their provisions until the conditions of peace were fulfilled, after
which the League would undertake supervision. Depending on
function, the commissions were located in Paris or on the spot.
Membership varied. Boundary commissions included the interested
parties plus one or several of the great powers. The Rhineland High
Commission consisted of the four occupying powers, Britain,
France, America and Belgium. The composition of military control
commissions to supervise disarmament varied but always included
France and Britain. The important Reparations Commission in
Paris included the three major European powers and America,
plus a fifth seat occupied by Belgium on German questions, Yugo-
slavia on east European questions, and Japan on naval questions.
These and other commissions were supervised by the Conference of
Ambassadors in Paris representing the five great powers (although

the American soon became an 'intermittent observer'[7] and Belgium was occasionally added on German questions). The Conference was charged with overseeing the implementation of the peace and resolving any tag-end problems which might arise.

The commissions encountered many difficulties. Some lacked sufficient authority. The Conference of Ambassadors soon collided with a council of the great powers, found its decision overturned, lost what authority it had possessed, and subsided into inconsequence. Most commissions were ill-equipped to enforce their decisions; they lacked automatic sanctions, especially any applicable by majority vote. As disagreements developed among commission members or major powers over interpretation of treaty clauses, there was no authoritative independent body to render a decision. Worse yet, the membership of several commissions shrank from five to four as America withdrew, and so the potential for deadlock increased.

The United States pursued no consistent course regarding the commissions during its erratic withdrawal, but the remaining American representatives quickly ceased to vote. The resultant dislocation of the peace structure was acute and, as a consequence, this structure never functioned as originally envisaged. The chair of the Saar Commission, intended for America, passed to France, to the dismay of German-speaking Saarlanders. The distortion of the Reparations Commission was even greater. As America's reparations claims were minuscule and she was the least interested party, she was originally to chair a five-member commission where deadlock would be impossible since abstention counted as a negative vote. Upon American withdrawal, France, the most interested party, claimed both the chair and the casting vote in case of deadlock accorded to chairmen of other commissions. Thus France could control the commission with the support of one other member. As Britain tended to offend Belgium regularly and Italy tended to support the stronger side, the vote was often three to one, and the second, casting vote was never used on a German issue, but its presence in reserve bolstered France's position. Moreover, whenever Britain refused to participate, the Reparations Commission found enforcement of its decisions difficult.

America was the only state with sufficient power (through use of the war debts issue, if in no other way) to serve as referee and force clear-cut decisions. In her absence implementation of the peace or a systematic revision of it might still have been possible had there been any agreement among the remaining powers concerned, but there was none. Britain and France agreed on almost nothing. France and Italy came to terms with Turkey, while Britain backed Greece virtually to the end. France supported Poland against Russia and in Silesia, while Britain emphatically did not. The interests of the two powers in Russia were competitive, not complementary. In late 1921 Lord Curzon went so far as to declare:

... the Foreign Office is only too painfully aware that in almost every quarter of the globe, whether it be Silesia or Bavaria or Hungary or the Balkans – Morocco or Egypt or Turkey or Mesopotamia – the representatives of France are actively pursuing a policy which is either unfriendly to British interests or, if not that, is consecrated to the promotion of a French interest which is inconsistent with ours.[8]

Beyond that, the British were distracted by Ireland and Empire while French interests centred primarily in Europe. On that continent France was nervous about the patent British desire to restore pre-war trade patterns with Germany and Russia, while Britain was equally nervous about the French air force and submarines.[9] Britain seriously debated whether the next war would be against France, and when an alliance with France was under consideration late in 1921, the chief argument in its favour was that, 'If, as some think, the most likely enemy is France herself, then, as long as the alliance lasted, such a danger would indeed be eliminated.'[10]

As the peace settlement crumbled, the fear-driven French became sticklers for at least a modicum of enforcement, while the British, who were having second thoughts about many aspects of the settlement, encouraged the crumbling process. Inevitably deadlock ensued and, with it, an opportunity for defeated powers to manoeuvre. Japan had neither the will nor the power to embroil herself in European squabbles. Italy was torn by internal strife and not genuinely a great power. The small states were dismayed but helpless. In terms of the peace structure, Belgium was the most important of these, and since she shared some aspects of both British and French views, she struggled to achieve the awkward compromises in German matters which followed. These only papered over the rift and postponed the breach which soon transformed many of the commissions and much of the settlement itself.

Beyond these difficulties lay others. Many of the mechanical inadequacies of the enforcement system derived from the false assumption that the treaties would be honoured and largely self-enforcing. But the Dutch refused to relinquish the Kaiser, and Germany did not surrender alleged war criminals. Nor did she disarm on schedule or meet reparations quotas. Austria could not and did not pay reparations. Poland did not accept her frontiers; Italian troops did not evacuate Fiume; and Turkey did not accept the Treaty of Sèvres. Nothing much happened. The will to enforce the treaties was lacking or at best divided. While Britain supported Greece, France had no inclination to detach troops from the Rhine to force Turkey to honour the Sèvres settlement. Similarly, Britain had no intention of supporting Poland in Silesia or of stopping her seizure of Vilna from Lithuania. Even when some agreement existed the fundamental problem remained. One boundary decision was six to one, but the dissenter was Germany, who kept the disputed territory because no power was prepared to enforce the transfer. The overriding difficulty was that the only effective vehicle of enforcement was force and, after four years of war, nobody was prepared to risk the possibility of more war.

As the treaties crumbled the commissions grew. Numerous special missions were sent to the trouble spots of eastern Europe and, as plebiscites were postponed and tensions mounted, supervisory teams became larger. German refusal to permit inspections often left military control commissions with little to do, but they remained in place. German refusal of border delimitations gave boundary commissions a new lease on life as precise frontiers remained undefined for years. A vast administrative structure developed in the occupied Rhineland, and the revision of the Turkish treaty generated new agencies. Above all the Reparations Commission swelled. As Austria reached financial collapse, Allied reparations claims were abandoned, but agencies subsidiary to the Reparations Commission proliferated in Paris and Vienna to supervise the loans which kept Austria alive. As Germany defaulted steadily, Turkey was substantially relieved of reparations, and the others paid in part, the Reparations Commission became a vast army retreating steadily into never-never-land and emitting a bewildering barrage of highly technical documents, with which the statesmen had neither the competence nor the desire to cope. Yet as the reparations question was fraught with political consequences, cope they did after a fashion.

The statesmen did desire to deal themselves with the main issues which soon came to include many secondary questions. In creating an elaborate peace structure the leaders had delegated much. Then they took a good deal back into their own hands. Many apparently minor problems involved national prestige, strategic alliances, imperial considerations, or the future pattern of international relations. Accordingly, the Premiers and Foreign Ministers met so often together that the immediate postwar period is sometimes called the era of international conferences. So many of these took place at expensive resorts that the French politican Raymond Poincaré spoke disparagingly of 'la politique des casinos'.[11]

Equally important were the unofficial conferences, usually in conjunction with League sessions. The League came into official being in 1920 and wandered from place to place (again, often resorts) until its buildings in Geneva were completed. While most statesmen soon recognised that the League's powers were illusory, their electorates often did not, and thus many European Foreign Ministers faithfully attended the regular meetings of the Assembly and Council. These afforded excellent opportunities for quiet diplomacy outside the formal sessions. Foreign Ministers whose countries were officially on poor terms arranged to have rooms in the same hotel and met privately, safe from the pressures of public opinion. Perhaps this opportunity for unofficial consultation was one of the League's more substantial contributions to the unsuccessful effort to create an enduring peace. Indeed, looking back after ten years of experience, a senior British official acknowledged that the League had few noteworthy achievements to its credit but remarked: 'If Monsieur A. has Herr B. and Signor C. to dinner – even a bad dinner – several times a year, the tone of the diplomatic correspondence between those three statesmen (to say nothing of their conversation) undergoes a change. Before the war this curious and general trait was never properly exploited.'[12]

While unofficial diplomacy was usually narrow in scope, especially in the early years, the formal conferences were far-ranging in agenda. These large-scale deliberations began in February 1920 and continued until their culmination at Locarno in October 1925. At first the sessions were largely devoted to completing the Treaty of Sèvres and the Near Eastern settlement, discussing the many problems arising from the Russian situation, and attempting to repair the treaties already in effect. By the time the last treaty was completed the earlier treaties were unravelling.

Apart from Turkey, the chief centres of revisionism were Hungary and Germany. Hungary occupied Slovakia in March 1919, but was brought to withdrawal by an Allied ultimatum. There was nervous talk in Paris of what to do if Hungary ignored Allied commands; however, the crisis passed without need for resort to force. Then Hungary invaded Romania in July 1919, but a vigorous Romanian counter-offensive in August swept the Magyars back into Hungary, toppled the Communist regime of Bela Kun, and led after elections to restoration of the monarchy with Admiral Miklos Horthy as Regent. Hungary threatened Slovakia again in 1920 during the Russo-Polish war, and twice in 1921 ex-Kaiser Karl tried to return to the Hungarian throne. These moves were defeated by energetic action, including military mobilisation, from Hungary's neighbours, led by Czechoslovakia. Thereafter Hungary subsided into truculence, implying that she hoped to march against one neighbour or another to regain lost territory at the first favourable moment. Continuing Hungarian irredentism together with the events of 1920 and 1921 led to the completion in 1921 of the Little Entente consisting of Czechoslovakia, Yugoslavia and Romania. This bloc had ties to France, Poland, Austria and Italy (despite continuing Italo-Yugoslav friction in the Adriatic), but its core was the three states immediately threatened by Hungarian revisionism.[13]

The Little Entente was a success and Hungarian revisionism failed because the three countries had agreed views on a common opponent, were energetically led by Czech foreign minister Édouard Beneš, and were prepared to use force if necessary. The name 'Little Entente' arose from a derisive Hungarian analogy to the greater Entente trying to cope with German revisionism. Beyond the names the two groups had little in common. What became known as the Western Entente in the interwar years derived from the Anglo-French Entente Cordiale of 1904 and the wartime alliance. In the postwar era, it consisted of Britain and France with the intermittent involvement of Italy and the participation of Belgium as junior partner. The Entente powers did not have agreed views, were not energetically led, and in the main were not prepared to use force. Thus German revisionism was far more successful than that of Hungary, and one of the key features of European history in the 1920s was the progressive dismantling of the Versailles Treaty.

German resistance to the treaty commenced as it took effect. On the rare occasions of Entente unity Germany had no success, but, more often, Anglo-French disagreement provided manoeuvring room for German efforts to modify the settlement. As Germany failed to fulfil treaty terms, notably on disarmament and reparations, military intervention was discussed at Entente conferences regularly from March 1920 onwards, but Germany was a great power and Britain was increasingly unwilling to contemplate any threat which might have to be made good. As early as April 1920 the French unilaterally occupied Frankfurt and three neighbouring towns in response to an unauthorised German army incursion into the demilitarised zone in the Ruhr valley. While the French action was effective, Britain protested loudly. Thereafter through conference after conference as German recalcitrance was discussed, France advocated an occupation of the Ruhr and Britain resisted. As treaty enforcement without such sanctions became increasingly problematic and the question of an occupation thus became increasingly immediate, the British became ever more resistant and an impasse in the Entente ensued.

Few conferences of the postwar years, whatever their formal agenda, concluded without a discussion of German reparations or German disarmament, or both. The disarmament question dragged on for years, as Germany simply did not meet the stringent treaty requirements. Similarly, the reparations question poisoned the air throughout the 1920s. The Versailles Treaty had provided for interim payments of 20 milliard* gold marks in cash and kind (coal, timber, chemicals, and so on) until the total liability could be set by the Reparations Commission. However, Germany did not meet her coal quotas. They were revised downward and still she did not meet them. Finally, at the Spa Conference in July 1920, the first postwar German meeting with the victors (at which a Ruhr occupation was seriously contemplated), the coal quotas were again revised and the shipments partially subsidised. At Spa, the Entente powers finally decided what the distribution of reparations would be (France 52 per cent, Britain and Empire 22 per cent,

---

* A British milliard is the equivalent of an American billion. The exchange rate was four gold marks to the dollar and twenty to the pound.

Italy 9·5 per cent, Belgium 8 per cent, Yugoslavia 3·5 per cent, and 5 per cent for the rest)[14] – when and if they could agree on the total liability.

The Entente reparations haggle moved back and forth across the Channel for many more months. France and Italy wanted as high a figure as possible while Britain, eager to restore her pre-war trade with Germany, fought for minimal payments. Eventually a Belgian compromise figure of 132 milliard gold marks plus the Belgian war debt was accepted and announced by the Reparations Commission on 27 April 1921 as the total liability of all the Central Powers combined. Public opinion in most receiver countries was dismayed by the smallness of the figure, but economists and statesmen knew it was far more than Germany could pay and knew also that the other Central Powers could pay little. Accordingly, at the London Conference of May 1921, an elaborate sleight of hand reduced the German debt to 50 milliard gold marks (including the unpaid balance of 12 milliard on the interim 20 milliard) to be paid over thirty-six years according to complex schedules for delivery of cash and kind.[15] The London Schedule of Payments was presented to Germany on 5 May 1921 in the form of a unanimous Entente ultimatum with an occupation of the Ruhr threatened. The French Premier, Aristide Briand, who was much the most moderate French leader of the era, had wanted, owing to the intense pressures of French opinion, to occupy the Ruhr immediately on the strength of German default on the interim payment, but Lloyd George insisted on awaiting Germany's response to the ultimatum.[16]

Faced with Entente unanimity and threats, Germany underwent the inevitable Cabinet crisis and then accepted the London Schedule of Payments. The first cash payment was met in full in the summer of 1921, partly because Entente sanctions imposed in March in an effort to evoke a satisfactory German reparations offer were still in effect. With the cash payment economic sanctions ended, but Entente occupation of a small area around Düsseldorf continued despite British objections. Germany made no further cash payments until after the Dawes Plan went into effect late in 1924. While coal and timber quotas were repeatedly revised downwards, they were never met in full. As a consequence the reparations quarrel continued. Instead of arguing over how much, the victors now debated whether to make Germany pay. Through conference after conference, plan after plan was debated without any resolution of the issue.

In the interim France had reacted to German intransigence and British resistance to sanctions. Most Frenchmen had always believed that the Versailles Treaty was barely adequate to ensure French security. Now that its erosion was evident, France sought allies. In July 1920 she badgered a reluctant Belgium into a limited military agreement and in February 1921 she signed a full alliance and military convention with Poland. These arrangements provided some security on the traditional invasion route into France and also a tie to a substantial, battle-seasoned army to Germany's east. Beyond that, French ties with Czechoslovakia had been close since the wartime efforts of Czech *émigrés* in Paris and these provided an informal link to the Little Entente. This link was formalised by a Franco-Czech treaty in January 1924,[17] thus affording France an ally on Germany's south as well as her west and east.

Such allies were of substantial military worth but they were not great powers. France had long recognised that the Anglo-American guarantee was defunct and had shown only sporadic interest in any bilateral Anglo-French arrangement. However, increasing German intransigence together with yet another squabble with Britain heightened French fear of isolation and thus her interest in a British tie.

The United States triggered the renewed attempt at Anglo-French *rapprochement* by returning briefly to the international scene and sponsoring the Washington Conference, which lasted from November 1921 until February 1922.[18] The purposes of this conference were several. One was to disengage Britain from her pre-war alliance with Japan. Canada in particular feared that some future Japanese–American clash in the Pacific would precipitate Anglo-American conflict. Another aim was to extract Japan from the Shantung peninsula and to settle a variety of Sino-Japanese questions pending since the war, including the Twenty-One Demands forced upon China by Japan in 1915. Both goals were achieved by sweeping new arrangements for the Far East. While Japan was a major power and China was in a state of anarchy with three competing governments, China had Entente support not available to her during the pressures of war, but now developing as Anglo-American concern grew over increasing Japanese power in the Pacific. Thus the Chinese were relieved of many Japanese infringements, and the Nine-Power Pact of 6 February 1922 affirmed (without commitment to defend) the independence and integrity of China along with an 'Open Door' for the trade of all nations and debarred future special concessions there. However, existing concessions continued, including the privileged Japanese position in Manchuria, and China was not restored to full sovereignty. The Anglo-Japanese alliance was submerged in an anodyne Four-Power Pact of Britain, France, America and Japan designed to preserve the *status quo* in the Pacific area.

The other major goal of the Washington Conference was naval disarmament. While the peace settlement had forcibly disarmed the defeated powers, it had also implied that universal disarmament should follow. The United States, potentially the world's greatest naval power but entering on fiscal conservatism, burdened with a two-ocean navy, and alarmed at Japan's rising strength, took the lead to limit the world's major navies. In the end the Five-Power Treaty of 6 February 1922 followed the American plan in most respects. Naval tonnage for capital ships was limited to 525,000 for Britain and America, 300,000 for Japan, and 175,000 for France and Italy. Thus Britain accepted equality with America and the mistress of the seas reigned no more, while France reluctantly accepted humiliating parity with Italy, the only power able eventually to increase her navy under the arrangement. The three greatest naval powers had to scrap existing vessels to meet the limits. There was to be no construction of capital ships whatever for ten years, then only replacement of ships more than twenty years old with strict limitations on tonnage and armaments, and in a national ratio of 10:10:6:3·5:3·5. The American desire to extend these arrangements to lesser ships ran foul of French intransigence on auxiliary vessels, particularly submarines. The Five-Power Treaty also banned further fortification of potential island bases in the western Pacific, a decision to the advantage of Japan, given her local superiority and lesser distances to cover. It was the hope of America that the treaty would end naval rivalry and imperial competition and create in their place a new system of international relations in the Far East complementary to the European-oriented western system of the League. The Pacific arrangement, like its European counterpart, foundered on the fallacy that all nations, whether dissatisfied, incarcerated in inferiority, or non-signatory, would abide indefinitely by self-denying ordinances.

Throughout the Washington Conference France was isolated and disgruntled. The quarrel with Britain over submarines was especially bitter, revealing a substantial residue of British distrust of France. Briand took alarm and upon his return home proposed an Anglo-French alliance to Lloyd George. While cautious, Lloyd George agreed that the matter could be added to the already crowded agenda for the Cannes Conference, due to open on 6 January 1922. This conference was expected to deal with several issues, including German reparations defaults and a British plan for a world-wide economic conference. During the Cannes meetings, however, Briand suddenly resigned in response to press and political attacks charging him with subservience to British policy.[19] Thus the Cannes Conference came to an abrupt end and experts in time concocted yet another reparations plan which papered over German default and avoided declaring it, for if it were declared, something would have to be done and there was no agreement on what to do.

As a consequence also, the negotiations for an Anglo-French alliance proved abortive. *En route* for home Lloyd George stopped in Paris to see Poincaré, the Premier designate, who was as narrowly rigid as Briand was flexible and whose obsession with Germany was nearly total. The ensuing stormy discussion of the proposed pact revealed clashing mentalities. Lloyd George argued that the pledged aid of the British Empire should suffice, while Poincaré demanded to know how many British divisions France would receive in how many days.[20] After this impasse, negotiations dragged on for some months. Britain offered a sweeping but unspecific guarantee against Germany in return for French concessions all over the globe. Poincaré found both the price and the ambiguity unattractive and soon let the matter drop.

The one item settled at Cannes before Briand's resignation was a plan for a major economic conference, eventually held at Genoa. This had been Lloyd George's own idea and Poincaré was unenthusiastic, but the commitment had been made and plans proceeded apace. Lloyd George's concern arose in part from the chaotic condition of European trade. Pre-war trade patterns had been disrupted not only by war but also by peace, as new boundaries, new tariff barriers, and new currencies inhibited the flow of goods. Inflation was rife across the continent and exporters were therefore reluctant to exchange valuable goods for increasingly valueless money. In western Europe reconstruction generated inflation and government deficits. In France alone 80 milliard francs* were expended by 1926 to repair the wartime ravages and restore industrial production. In eastern Europe currencies were unstable and economic nationalism rampant, as each new country sought self-sufficiency and protected infant industries, thus pricing its goods out of international markets. As Czechoslovakia had an industrial surplus and Hungary an agricultural surplus, an exchange of products would have made economic sense but, given the constant hostility between the two countries, it was politically impossible, and Hungary launched her own steel industry. In most east-European countries, land reform broke up vast estates into small, less efficient farms, thus reducing the agricultural surplus available for export. Further east, Russia coped with rampant inflation, the ravages of civil war, and political stabilisation. She did so in political isolation and her involvement in international trade was scant.

As the war had done much physical and financial damage to Europe as a whole, European-wide industrial capacity had decreased sharply, non-European competition in world markets had increased considerably, much foreign exchange had been lost, and governments were burdened with huge domestic and foreign debts along with heavy expenses for pensions. Furthermore, the impoverished continent had now to support more people on less production as restrictive American legislation choked off the swollen pre-war stream of European emigrants to the New World. Overpopulation soon became acute in eastern Europe, depressing the economy of the region and rendering it less able to buy western Europe's industrial goods. Signs of stagnation quickly appeared in the west. Clearly Europe's economic circulatory system needed restorative measures.

Lloyd George was even more concerned about the parlous economic condition of Britain. Her industrial plant was war-battered and obsolete; British goods could not compete in world markets or even in British markets; foreign trade languished; unemployment was high and strikes frequent. In 1920 American iron was underselling Scottish iron on the Glasgow market, while Belgian iron sold at about half the price of the local product. At

* That is to say about 64 milliard marks, $16 milliard, or £3·2 milliard.

the same time, most west-European countries and the British colonies were reducing purchases of high-priced British goods. Worse yet, in 1911–13 on average Germany absorbed 8·3 per cent of British exports, but in 1920 only 1·5 per cent and in 1921 2·4 per cent.[21] Faced with such figures Lloyd George hoped that restoration of pre-war patterns of European trade would alleviate some of Britain's economic distress. While badly in need of a foreign policy success to bolster his sagging coalition, Lloyd George was genuinely eager to bring Russia and Germany back into economic circulation and also genuinely afraid that those two political pariahs might join together in an anti-western bloc.

There had already been British negotiations with Russia in 1920 and a limited Anglo-Russian trade treaty in 1921. Re-entry of Russia into the European family had been sharply limited, however, by the unwillingness of Britain and other nations to grant *de jure* recognition to Lenin's government, by Soviet repudiation of Tsarist debts to western countries, and by Russian nationalisation of foreign private property. Lloyd George hoped to resolve these difficulties in a widely representative conference which would so revitalise European trade that the Franco-German clash and the unresolvable reparations issue would shrink into insignificance. Exclusion from the agenda of reparations and war debts, two questions deeply affecting the economies of most European states, had been the price of French participation but none the less Lloyd George remained optimistic. The Russians were considerably less hopeful but delighted to be included in European diplomacy for the first time since 1917, while the Germans were glad of an opportunity to participate in something other than an adversary relationship to the Western Entente.

Lloyd George's fears of Russo–German rapprochement proved justified. During the first week of the Genoa Conference, which opened on 10 April 1922, Lloyd George assiduously courted the Russians. Germany took alarm and thus chose this moment to sign the previously drafted Treaty of Rapallo (a resort near Genoa), which burst upon a startled world on 16 April, indicating that the russophiles had won over the westerners in the German Foreign Ministry. By its terms, Germany granted Russia *de jure* recognition and cancelled all debt claims, provided that Russia did not compensate other claimants, a proviso with major implications for the conference itself. The treaty provided for close economic relations and mutual most-favoured-nation treatment.[22] There were immediate rumours of secret military clauses. These did not exist, as a secret Russo-German military collaboration had already begun in 1921, but the Rapallo rapprochement led inevitably to its rapid expansion.

It was a marriage of enormous convenience. Russia had the raw materials Germany needed, while Germany had the manufactured goods and technological sophistication Russia wished desperately to acquire. Russia also had the space Germany wanted. On the Russian plains, far from the prying eyes of military control commissions, Germany could and did build factories, produce the airplanes, poison gases, and tanks forbidden by the Versailles Treaty, test them, and train military personnel, both German and Russian, in their use. While this mutually beneficial arrangement had its ups and downs, it flourished throughout the twenties and to a lesser degree until the advent of Hitler.[23]

In the short run the Treaty of Rapallo wrecked the Genoa Conference. Lloyd George struggled on for five more weeks, trying to find a way to reintegrate Russia into the European economic structure. The chief stumbling block was the substantial pre-war western investment in Russia. The Soviet government had nationalised all foreign enterprises without compensation. No government had done this before; the rights of private property remained sacrosanct throughout the western world. Naturally the shock and outrage were intense. At Genoa western leaders, prodded by infuriated investors, still sought restitution, while Russia offered only a hazy possibility of some compensation. The British tried to bring others at least part way to the Russian view, but when the Paris press floated reports that British interests were negotiating to obtain pre-war Franco-Belgian oil concessions in Russia,[24] Poincaré had the excuse he sought to stand adamant. The Conference concealed its failure by delegating its problems to an expert committee at The Hague, which achieved nothing.

With the failure at Genoa the old problem of Germany returned to the fore. The twin issues of reparations and disarmament remained unabated, but the chief focus was on reparations. The arrangements patched together in the aftermath of Cannes had relieved Germany temporarily of cash payments and reduced coal and timber quotas, but, unless something were done, the London Schedule of Payments would resume effect on 1 January 1923. By mid-July 1922 Germany had requested a full moratorium* on cash payments for the remainder of 1922 and all of 1923 and 1924. British experts felt that Germany needed a longer and more sweeping moratorium, covering kind as well as cash, while the French were unwilling to consider any extended moratorium without seizing something (customs revenues, state forests, tax receipts, or whatever) to ensure that Germany would eventually resume payment. A technical device deferred the 1922 cash payments, but some more substantial arrangement would be necessary before 1 January 1923. There was no agreement on what it should be. Thus the dispute over reparations dominated the remainder of 1922.[25]

By this time the reparations question was entangled with several others. One was German economic and monetary health. Successive German governments claimed that reparations demands were destroying the German economy and currency. While Germany, who had emerged from the war and the peace with most of her industrial strength intact, was economically healthy, her monetary ailments were serious. Germany had ended the war with the mark worth half its pre-war value. Thereafter the inflation of prices and depreciation of the currency had continued at a rapid if erratic rate. A clear conjunction had developed between Entente reparations demands or payment deadlines and sudden dramatic inflationary lurches of the mark. Germany claimed that reparations demands caused the dismaying depreciation. Both British and French experts at the time thought the reverse was true: that Germany was deliberately destroying her currency to escape reparations. However, they drew opposite conclusions. The British felt that since Germany had succeeded in destroying her currency, she must be granted a long moratorium and an extended opportunity for financial reconstruction.[26] France objected to awarding the requested moratorium as a bad conduct prize and feared that reparations, once halted, would never be resumed.

By this time also, the conjunction between reparations and war debts had become almost absolute. Originally there was no connection between the reparations Germany owed for the damage done in France and Belgium (and the other less valid claims elsewhere) and the enormous debts owed to America by the wartime Allies either directly or through the agency of Britain, who had served as Allied broker for American loans. Moreover, most Allied

* Legal authorisation to debtors to postpone payment.

countries carried huge domestic debts as a consequence of the war and some were incurring further large debts to repair the wartime ravages. The victors were taxing their citizenry far more heavily than the vanquished. On top of that loomed the American debts.* The American people took the view that a debt is a debt and must be repaid in full with interest. Accordingly, the American Congress took the same view and, by 1922, it was clear that war debt relief was not a practical possibility. The money had to come from somewhere and the only available source was German reparations. In an effort to break the log-jam, on 1 August 1922 Britain issued the Balfour Note urging all-around cancellation of reparations and war debts, but, since America's attitude made that impossible, declaring that Britain would ask from her debtors only what she must pay to her American creditors. This proposal met with a hostile reception from British financial circles, America, and France. Both the latter refused to accept the connection between reparations and war debts, while Poincaré indicated that, for France, more was involved in reparations than money.

Another factor which sharply exacerbated the reparations crisis of late 1922 was that the British were distracted and gave it little thought. French interests were firmly centred on Germany and Germany's immediate neighbours. Britain was interested in everything, and everything was happening at once. The British economic situation, unlike that of France, remained grave and gave impetus to British desires for reconstruction of the German economy. Germany was in fact a competitor in such sickly British industries as steel, shipbuilding, and coal export, and German distress redounded to British benefit. But the British held fast to Lloyd George's nostalgic belief that a healthy Germany in a healthy Europe would alleviate Britain's deep-seated economic problems.

There were also Lloyd George's own problems. His Greco-Tur-

---

* In round figures, war debts to America in terms of original indebtedness (before interest multiplied the totals) were as follows:

Britain	$ almost	5	milliard (billion)	£ almost	1	milliard
France	over	4	milliard	over	800	million
Italy	over	2	milliard	over	400	million
Belgium	over	400	million	over	80	million
Poland	over	200	million	over	40	million
Czechoslovakia	almost	200	million	almost	40	million

and down the scale to Liberia which owed $26,000 (£5200). U.S. Treasury figures, *World Almanac* (1974) p. 510.

kish policy was winding to its disastrous close and a triumphant Kemal, having expelled the Greeks from Smyrna and having persuaded France and Italy to withdraw, was on the brink of open warfare with British forces at Chanak on the Asian side of the Dardanelles. An armistice was eventually arranged on 11 October, but the long crisis distracted Britain from the European scene and led to the fall of Lloyd George's coalition. He was replaced by the ailing Andrew Bonar Law at the head of a Conservative government. An election ensued, providing further distraction, along with a strenuous but successful effort to arrange payment of the American debt (on America's terms). Above all a new Prime Minister was pitched into the height of the reparations crisis.

This crisis was predictable long in advance, but British Cabinets, distracted by Turkey and domestic politics, never substantially discussed the issue throughout the autumn and early winter. Bonar Law, lacking Lloyd George's long experience in such matters, failed to see the opportunities open to him. He ignored Belgium's frantic appeals to avert a breakdown of the Entente and a Ruhr occupation, overlooked signs that Poincaré himself was searching for a solution short of marching into the Ruhr,[27] and disregarded the possibilities presented by the termination of a long Italian political crisis with the advent of Benito Mussolini, who ardently wanted attention on the international scene. He failed to see that France never acted against Germany when the rest of the Entente stood firm against her, and he unnecessarily offended Belgium and Italy, sending both to France's side. British leaders similarly failed to see that Germany never resisted when the entire Entente stood together against her, only when Anglo-French disagreement provided room for manoeuvre. The British reasoned that nothing should be asked of Germany because Germany would refuse and then something would have to be done. The only thing that could be done was an occupation of the Ruhr valley, and Britain was by definition against that. So Britain insisted on a four-year moratorium without guarantees, while France, feeling that the Versailles Treaty was at stake, demanded both Entente unity and substantial guarantees.

Through Entente conferences and Reparations Commission wrangles, the crisis deepened. At the end of the year Germany was in massive default on timber deliveries, and the default was formally declared over strenuous British opposition, although the Reparations Commission took no further action. Germany was defaulting regularly on her monthly coal quotas,[28] and that question would loom in January for perhaps the last time as France decided that enough was enough. Also in January there must be a new reparations plan – and there was none.

On 2 January 1923 the Entente powers and Germany converged on Paris. Everybody except the Belgians brought a plan and each of these was published at once, thus inflaming public opinion everywhere. The German proposal, foreshadowing Locarno, offered a Rhineland pact as a diversion from reparations default. Poincaré declined to be diverted. The French and Italian plans stressed Entente unity and limited economic sanctions, although the French indicated that, lacking unity, they would take more drastic action. Bonar Law brushed these aside and insisted that the British plan[29] was the only possible basis for discussion. This was merely a revision of a plan previously rejected by France. It would have destroyed all Belgian benefits from reparations, given Germany a four-year moratorium on cash and kind without any guarantees, required open cancellation (a politically difficult act) of the more ephemeral portions of Germany's ostensible obligation, reduced and reconstructed the Reparations Commission to destroy France's preponderance therein, given Britain a veto over any punitive measures against Germany in the event of future default, and given Britain a free hand to dictate Entente policy in all non-German reparations. As this plan would have meant the practical end of reparations, no continental politician could have accepted it and remained in office. None did, and the conference quickly dissolved in deadlock.

On 9 January 1923 the Reparations Commission declared the coal default by a vote of three to one and, on the strength of it, by the same vote decided to occupy the Ruhr. On 11 January French, Belgian and Italian technicians charged with procuring the coal entered the Ruhr, protected by small contingents of French and Belgian troops. At the eleventh hour the British, who voiced their disapproval of the occupation openly, considered whether to let the French mount it on the railways running through the British Rhineland zone into the Ruhr. Although it could have been accomplished in no other way and thus the British could have blocked the occupation, consent was given. Bonar Law dreaded a breach with France, not recognising that it had already arrived. Later, as both the occupation and British opposition to it swelled, Britain thoughtfully readjusted Rhineland zonal boundaries to transfer a key rail-way to French control so that France could handle its increasing Ruhr traffic.[30]

Throughout the long Ruhr crisis, Poincaré misjudged the Ruhr operation and the British misjudged Poincaré. Both errors exacer-bated and prolonged the crisis, to the cost of almost all countries concerned. Poincaré had struggled to avoid drastic action, but had been driven to it by the French right and inadvertently by the British.[31] A man of much ability but no imagination, he thought he could simply send in a few engineers and collect the coal, although Belgian leaders told him otherwise often enough. As the German government called for passive resistance and financed it from the empty German exchequer[32] to the utter ruination of the mark, French and Belgian troops poured into the Ruhr, which was sealed off from the rest of Germany. The industrial heart of Ger-many ceased to beat while Frenchmen and Belgians ran the rail-ways and mined the coal. Very quickly, Italy and Belgium lost heart and sought a way out, but Poincaré hung grimly on.

The British leaders never understood why. They could not comprehend French fear of Germany and thought Poincaré was being vindictive. They could not accept the simple fact that France needed the coal, her demands having greatly increased in conse-quence of German destruction of her mines in 1918 and the reac-quisition of the Lorraine iron fields, a need only partially filled by the Saar output. They failed to recognise that France urgently needed the money as reconstruction was being financed by borrow-ing and the franc was becoming increasingly precarious. Beyond that they could not see that what was at stake for France was the survival of the Versailles Treaty and indeed the victory in the war. Poincaré well knew that in occupying the Ruhr he had played the last trump and that there was no other. He had to win on this card or go down to defeat to a larger, industrially stronger, more popu-lous Germany with a higher birth-rate, boding ill for the future. Had Britain committed herself firmly to either side, the Ruhr episode would have ended quickly, but Britain balanced in the middle, unwilling to break with France or to discipline Germany, and kept trying futilely to bring the warring giants together. Lost in technicalities, the British leaders never realised that they were watching an extension of the First World War. Unfortunately it was to prove in some respects as costly and inconclusive as the war itself.

In the short run nobody suffered financially from the Ruhr crisis except the German people. The British economy improved as the chief competitor disappeared from European markets, although the British never admitted their profits even to themselves. British officials, blinded by their assumption that the Ruhr occupation was an economic disaster to Britain, insisted that there was no connection between the occupation and a significant drop in unemployment. They saw no correlation between employment figures and a total increase in exports, especially in coal and pig iron, along with heavier demands on British shipping, as continental buyers, denied the Ruhr's products, turned to British substitutes.[33] France and Belgium profited also, slowly at first and then very considerably, although the British denied that reality by comparing the Ruhr receipts to the London Schedule of Payments, ignoring the fact that the London Schedule was defunct and that the choice had been, at British insistence, between the Ruhr receipts and nothing. The German government and state enterprises paid off their domestic debts with worthless inflation marks, while leading German entrepreneurs, such as Hugo Stinnes, who had close ties to the business cabinet of Wilhelm Cuno, took advantage of the situation to buy up failing firms and corner a startling percentage of German national wealth. While the German working class suffered from the runaway inflation, the middle class suffered more, both financially and psychologically. However, the demoralisation of the German middle class, paving the way for the advent of Hitler, is another story outside the scope of this book.[34]

After an increasingly bitter struggle Poincaré's trump won. In August 1923, Gustav Stresemann became German Chancellor, and in September he called off the passive resistance. Franco-Belgian profits soared[35] and their forces remained in the Ruhr. While the more stringent aspects of the occupation were gradually relaxed, there remained the problems of reforming the German currency (rapidly accomplished by Stresemann), extracting the French from the Ruhr, and creating a new reparations plan. The latter two tasks took nearly two years. When the job was done, Poincaré was in eclipse and his victory appeared hollow indeed.

After September 1923 the battle continued, but now Britain and Germany joined forces to minimise the effect of the Ruhr occupation, while Poincaré struggled to preserve France's victory. As American and Belgian pressure was added to Anglo-German efforts, Poincaré's isolation increased, the franc sagged dangerously, and the eventual outcome became inevitable, particularly since American bankers were in a position to impose conditions for both the loan France urgently needed and the loans to Germany essential to any new reparations plan. None the less Poincaré held out stubbornly, in turn delaying an easement of the occupation, supporting Rhenish separatism, and staving off a comprehensive reparations settlement which was bound to lead to a less satisfactory situation for France.

Poincaré's extreme slowness in easing the rigours of the occupation was one of several factors leading to separatist outbreaks in the occupied Rhineland at the end of 1923. France had tried both by diplomacy and by backing Rhenish separatism to detach the Rhineland from Germany in 1919. Now another opportunity presented itself. Poincaré knew that the Ruhr must eventually be evacuated, but if in the meantime he could detach the Rhineland, victory would be lasting. Thus France openly supported a ragtag batch of incompetent and unimpressive separatists. However, a premature separatist outbreak at Aachen in the Belgian zone in October 1923 was easily suppressed by the Belgian authorities, demonstrating that separatism had little popular support. Thereafter, a French-backed Rhenish republic at Coblenz had a short and squabbly life while an autonomous government in the Palatinate lasted until February 1924 when British threats of public exposure forced Poincaré to withdraw the conspicuous French support which kept the movement alive.[36]

As separatism collapsed Poincaré tried to delay a reparations settlement, but pressures from all the powers were too much for him. President Calvin Coolidge indicated in October 1923 that American citizens could participate unofficially in a committee of experts, thus making possible the American financial support vital to the success of any new reparations scheme. Despite much foot-dragging by France, a committee under the chairmanship of Charles G. Dawes, an American banker, began work in January 1924. The Dawes Report, written largely in its technical aspects by Sir Josiah Stamp of Britain and Emile Franqui of Belgium and in its political arrangements by Owen D. Young of America, was issued in April 1924. The Plan operated at two levels: technically it was very precise and politically it was totally ambiguous, largely because political factors would determine its fate. No government liked the Dawes Plan much, for widely varying reasons, but each accepted it in full, the French and Germans only after intense British pressure, because there was no alternative.

The Dawes Plan[37] called for complete reorganisation of German finances with some foreign supervision, sweeping tax reform, a large international loan to Germany, and an agent-general for reparations in Berlin to oversee a complex administrative structure. An American, S. Parker Gilbert, held this key post throughout the history of the Dawes Plan. By including occupation costs, commission expenses, and all miscellaneous charges in German payments, the reparations total was effectively reduced, although by how much was unclear because the duration of the plan was unspecified. Germany would pay almost no reparations for two years, increasing amounts for two years, and 2500 milliard marks for one year. Thereafter Germany would pay 2500 milliard marks plus a percentage based on a complex index of German prosperity. Under the Dawes Plan, Germany always met her payments almost in full (thanks largely to a flood of American investment), but by the time the 2500 milliard mark year was reached, Germany sought and gained another downward revision. From the start Germany viewed the plan as a temporary expedient to remove the French from the Ruhr and keep reparations minimal. Revision as soon as payments became onerous was taken for granted in Germany.[38] The French suspected as much but, deep in financial crisis and urgently in need of Anglo-American financial aid, could do nothing.

While the Dawes Plan itself was quickly accepted, there remained reconstruction of the Reparations Commission, extraction of the French from the Ruhr, and a variety of agreements necessary to put the plan into effect. Since most of these arrangements constituted substantial revisions of the Versailles Treaty, a large international conference was necessary. Before it was held in London during July and August 1924, Poincaré had fallen, defeated largely as a result of his diplomatic isolation. He was replaced in June 1924 by Édouard Herriot, who was both inexperienced and eager for a settlement. In addition, in January 1924, Ramsay MacDonald had become the first Labour Prime Minister in British history. Also inexperienced and eager for a settlement, MacDonald took close personal charge of British foreign policy, and the 1924 London Conference was his triumph, eased to its conclusion by his engagingly informal style. While Herriot and MacDonald were startlingly different from their predecessors, the shifts in British and French policies were barely perceptible. Both men were bound by national interests and shaky parliamentary majorities. Yet the change of heart and of style as both men stressed pleasantness provided enough manoeuvring space to achieve a settlement.

In London the Entente powers settled matters among themselves and then negotiated with Germany. In this latter stage Anglo-French disagreement gave the wily Stresemann an opportunity to gain concessions. He achieved much. Arrangements were made to implement the Dawes Plan in full, to end the economic occupation of the Ruhr almost at once, and to end a reduced military occupation in a year. The powers of the Reparations Commission were substantially reduced with an appeal to arbitration in the absence of unanimity or the presence of German protest, the addition of a private American citizen whenever declaration of default was under consideration, and provisions to make future sanctions against default virtually impossible.[39] These final provisions were necessary to gain endorsement by the American banking firm, J. P. Morgan, of large loans to Germany which would last twenty-five years, whatever happened to the Dawes Plan.[40] All governments concerned ratified the London settlement quickly. The only protest, purely *pro forma*, came from Germany, the chief beneficiary.

By the time the last French troops left the Ruhr in August 1925 it was clear that France had won the battle but lost the war. Gone was France's commanding position in a powerful Reparations Commission; gone was any hope of detaching the Rhineland or ever occupying the Ruhr again; gone were the Ruhr receipts, rapid reparations in the future, and sanctions against default. France had not only failed to enforce the peace which she considered minimal to her security; she had had to accept substantial revision of the peace to the advantage of what she considered to be her enemy. Moreover, as those last troops returned to France, it was evident that the revision of the peace already in progress would continue at an accelerating pace.

3 The Revision of the Peace

THE 1924 reparations settlement constituted a major revision of the Versailles Treaty in that the Reparations Commission was reorganised while both its powers and German payments were sharply reduced. By the time this scheme was achieved, there had been other revisions of the 1919 settlement as well. Most of the reparations provisions of the Paris treaties had been jettisoned. Austrian and Turkish reparations had been abandoned altogether. Hungary had been granted a virtual moratorium on all except small coal deliveries, while Bulgarian reparations had been scaled down to a more realistic 550 million gold francs plus a lump-sum payment of 25 million francs for occupation costs. Despite the reduction of reparations to a trickle, most European countries were facing facts and embarking on prolonged negotiations toward settlement of their American debts on long-term payment schemes. There remained a correlation between these plans and reparations schedules as European countries came to view reparations largely as a means to pay war debts.

There had been territorial revision as well, both *de jure* and *de facto*. The entire Turkish treaty had been revised to the advantage of Turkey, while the Washington Conference had undone one of Japan's two solid gains of 1919 and had partially rearranged the Far Eastern settlement to China's benefit. In Europe, Germany was allowed to retain some disputed border territories, although not those she wanted most. Poland's Russian frontier had settled far to the east of where the experts thought it should be, and her seizure of Vilna from Lithuania was accepted as permanent since nobody other than Lithuania was prepared to resort to force, while the retaliatory Lithuanian occupation of Memel was successful, thanks largely to its timing just as France was entering the Ruhr in January 1923. Although the Free City of Danzig had come into being, there was friction over Polish use of the port facilities, and Poland was building its own port at Gdynia. After open warfare

and an inconclusive plebiscite in 1921, upper Silesia had been par-
titioned on a line displeasing to both Poland and Germany. While
Germany retained the lion's share, Poland took the more economically lucrative part.

Further south, by 1924, Italy's seizure of Fiume had been recognised, and Yugoslavia had in turn taken advantage of Greece's
defeat by the Turks to gain substantial port rights at Salonica.
Yugoslavia had lost territory to Austria in the Klagenfurt plebiscite,
but had been permitted several frontier rectifications at Bulgarian
expense. She had also occupied northern Albania, while Greek
forces held eastern areas assigned to Albania by the Conference of
Ambassadors, but in the end both occupants bowed to threats from
the great powers. By the end of 1924, the Greco-Albanian frontier
had been delimited and the Yugoslav–Albanian border was in the
process of settlement. Greece gained a little over 1913 boundaries
but not much; Yugoslavia nothing at all. Here as elsewhere action
or the lack thereof by the major powers settled the issue. By the
middle twenties the Balkan borders had finally been established
except that between Russia and Romania, as the Soviet Union
would not recognise Romania's acquisition of Bessarabia despite
Romania's continuing effective occupation.

In the early twenties Russia concentrated chiefly upon ridding
herself of foreign troops and civil war, and upon reorganising the
ravaged country in the communist mode. Gradually, however,
after her abortive debut at the Genoa Conference, Russia reappeared on the international scene as western governments reluctantly faced the fact that the Marxist experiment would survive.
Until 1924 the Soviet government had gained *de jure* recognition
only from countries bordering upon her (except Romania), invariably through treaties delimiting the common frontier, and from
Germany in the Treaty of Rapallo. In 1924 the barrier broke. The
new Italian Premier Benito Mussolini, whose country had few pre-
war investments in Russia to consider, opened negotiations in 1923
but his desire to lead the way was frustrated by MacDonald's
precipitous recognition of the Russian regime on 1 February 1924.
Italy followed within a week, France in October. In the course of
1924 the Scandinavian monarchies and most central European
countries followed suit, abandoning many claims of pre-war
investors. In other countries the capitalist creed and the claims of
private property proved strong enough to prevent recognition. At

the end of 1924 Belgium and Holland still held out, as did America until 1933. The Bessarabian issue prevented Romanian recognition, while Japan delayed until 1925 out of reluctance to evacuate northern Sakhalin until guaranteed oil concessions there. Embarrassing incidents ensured that Switzerland, the citadel of finance, and the Vatician, citadel of religion, stood aloof.

As the Soviet Union resumed normal diplomatic relations with most countries and comrade ambassadors appeared in western capitals, Russia's diplomatic re-emergence was distinctly partial. Russia's own concerns were primarily domestic: reconstruction, economic development, and the internal power struggle after Lenin's death in January 1924 leading to the dictatorship of Joseph Stalin from 1927 on. Besides, capitalist countries remained wary and there was little serious discussion of inviting Russia to join the League of Nations. Even more than Germany, whose possible membership was discussed occasionally, Russia remained something of a pariah. None the less, most western countries wanted trade treaties with the Marxist regime as the harmony between Russian resources and western technology was self-evident. Several such treaties were signed, to the mutual benefit of both parties as western engineers aided in the modernisation of Russia and Soviet raw materials flowed west. Yet the country which had tried longest and hardest to reintegrate Russia into the European economy failed to achieve a sweeping trade treaty, thanks to the alleged activities of a new entity on the international scene.

Britain, plagued with deepening economic depression, had been struggling to revive the Russian trade since 1920,[1] and MacDonald pursued this goal as doggedly as Lloyd George had done. A treaty had been agreed but not ratified when on 25 October 1924 the Zinoviev letter appeared in the British press. This purported to be a directive from Gregory Zinoviev, head of the Comintern (Third or Communist International, so-called to distinguish it from the continuing Second or moderate socialist International led by Emile Vandervelde of Belgium), to British communist leaders, ordering them 'to stir up the masses of the British proletariat, to bring into movement the army of unemployed proletarians' to assure ratification of the treaty.[2]

The Comintern, formed in March 1919 to further world revolution, had fostered the Berlin and Bavarian communist movements of 1919, backed Bela Kun's short-lived Hungarian regime, tried to create a real 'red revolution' in the Ruhr in 1920, and contributed to the forced inclusion of the Armenian republic in the Soviet Union. It had created a communist party in China in 1921, apparently involved itself in an uprising in the Rand of South Africa in 1922, and engaged in a Bulgarian revolution in 1923. The Comintern tried to take advantage of the Ruhr crisis of 1923 by planning a German national uprising and by seizing brief control of Saxony and Thuringia. It had also taken direction of most national communist parties in the world.[3] While ostensibly an independent organisation of like-minded groups (as the Second International actually was), the Comintern was widely recognised to be an agency of the Russian Communist Party charged in the early twenties with undertaking the propaganda campaigns and rough work attendant upon world revolution while the Soviet government, with Gregory Chicherin as Commissar of Foreign Affairs, posed as the model of propriety in its quest for diplomatic recognition.

By 1924 the Comintern had largely abandoned immediate world revolution in favour of infiltrating moderate socialist parties and dictating the policies of foreign communist parties according to Russian requirements (usually to the detriment of the popularity of communism in the countries concerned) but, by then, most westerners were prepared to believe anything of it. Earlier exhortations by Zinoviev urging Islamic peoples to launch a holy war against British imperialism[4] lingered to strengthen the suspicions of the average Englishman. While the Zinoviev letter may well have been a forgery as both Zinoviev and the Soviet government claimed, its publication helped to ensure the defeat of the Labour government in the British election of 29 October 1924, the advent of a Conservative ministry under Stanley Baldwin with Austen Chamberlain as Foreign Secretary, and the abandonment of all efforts toward enlarging the Russian trade until MacDonald returned to power in 1929 and completed a more limited Anglo-Russian treaty in 1930. In the internal Russian power struggle after Lenin's death, the Comintern subsided as well, except in China where it remained influential until 1927.

It was the Fascist Mussolini, an ex-socialist and a conservative anti-communist, who led the way to recognition of Soviet Russia despite the problem of private property and the activities of the Comintern. It was Mussolini as well who revealed that another aspect of the peace had already been revised or, more accurately, had always been an illusion. Upon his accession to power in 1922 Mussolini had faced Italy's perennial problem of trying to be a great power while lacking the wherewithal, particularly in industrial resources. Thus he soon revealed a penchant for dramatic foreign-policy escapades where some glory could be collected on the cheap, but he had no heart at all for major ventures where much had to be risked. Grabbing Fiume and imposing a virtual protectorate in 1926 on hapless Albania, then in a state of civil war, made him a hero in Italy, but his erratic course in the 1923 Ruhr crisis and later at Locarno demonstrated his nervousness. In 1923, in the Corfu incident, Mussolini engaged in an adventure precisely to his taste and, at the same time, demonstrated the helplessness of the League to enforce the peace when anything remotely resembling a major power objected.

In August 1923 one of the numerous boundary commissions sent forth by the Conference of Ambassadors was delimiting the Greco-Albanian frontier when several of its staff, including Italian General Enrico Tellini, were mysteriously murdered on Greek soil. Mussolini, who had been looking for an excuse for action, immediately dispatched an ultimatum to Greece reminiscent of that from Austria to Serbia in 1914. Greece, battered by the Turkish defeat, flooded with refugees from Anatolia, and in the midst of a cabinet crisis, accepted the more reasonable Italian demands, rejected the rest, and proposed that the matter be referred to the League. Mussolini's response was to bombard and occupy the strategic Greek isle of Corfu commanding the entrance to the Adriatic Sea. Greece thereupon appealed to the League Council. Before it could act the Conference of Ambassadors demanded an inquiry into the death of its agents. Greece indicated willingness to accept its decisions as well. Mussolini threatened indefinite occupation of Corfu if the League intervened in response to the request of its Greek member; he much preferred the Conference of Ambassadors where the decision would essentially be taken by only three powers, of which Italy was one and France, badly in need of continued Italian support in the Ruhr, was another.[5] Led by the smaller states who were beneficiaries of the peace settlement and who thus wanted to maintain both it and as much League protection for small powers as possible, the League made a genuine effort to deal with the Corfu crisis, but Mussolini held firm. When the League produced a compromise solution, it was overridden by the Conference of *failure of League to resolve*

Ambassadors, a puny body of itself but an instrument of the great powers. The Ambassadors imposed heavy financial penalties on Greece, whose culpability was never established; Italy then evacuated Corfu. While Mussolini's original intent had been permanent occupation, he chose to take the profit and pacify European opinion in order to forestall support to Yugoslavia on the eve of his Fiume coup.[6]

The League Council considered certain implications of the Corfu episode and concluded that the League was not obligated to investigate a serious dispute 'likely to lead to a rupture'[7] in response to a request by a member and could not act at all if settlement through other channels was being attempted. Further, measures of coercion not intended as acts of war need not necessarily be considered violations of the Covenant. *Force majeure* was given a free hand. Mussolini was well pleased, but the League had failed its first test and had paved the way for future failures.

These came quickly in another sphere but for the same reason: the League was so much weaker than the powers which dominated it. In 1923 and 1924 the League made two attempts to achieve real peace by linking security and disarmament. Few further steps toward general disarmament had followed the Washington Naval Conference, and French fears regarding her security were an obvious barrier to reductions of military and air forces on the European continent. In July 1922, when negotiations toward an Anglo-French pact were lapsing, Lord Robert Cecil (who generally represented either Britain or South Africa at Geneva but who in any event was a power unto himself, impervious to Foreign Office direction) proposed a scheme to provide the security which would make disarmament possible. Out of this grew the Draft Treaty of Mutual Assistance laid before the League Assembly in September 1923. The Draft Treaty obligated all members to come to the aid of a victim of aggression (although military action was not required on another continent) with the Council allocating specific responsibilities. Regional arrangements to keep the peace were authorised under League supervision and provision was made for an elaborate disarmament scheme to follow, including quotas.[8] Most European states, led by France, approved the Draft Treaty, although some with reservations, but Britain, partly in response to pressure from the Empire, rejected the plan on 5 July 1924. Canada in particular had no wish to assume an obligation to wage war on the United States, or even to engage in economic sanctions against her southern neighbour upon whom her economy depended heavily.

This episode indicated clearly the conflict in British policy between continental interests and imperial ties. To complicate matters, while the Dominions nominally had no control over their own foreign policies, they had obtained *de facto* control by 1918, a fact made evident by their presence at the 1919 peace conference and their sometimes strident pursuit at Paris of their own interests. This situation was not formalised until the Statute of Westminster of 1931, which transformed the British Empire into the British Commonwealth of Nations, but in fact throughout the twenties the Dominions had their own seats at Geneva and British treaties specified that they would not be bound without their consent. Since British military manpower was limited without Dominion support, they could and did exercise considerable influence over the extent of British commitments.

With the onus for the defeat of the Draft Treaty on his shoulders, MacDonald sought a new scheme. His efforts in conjunction with Herriot led to the Geneva Protocol for the Pacific Settlement of International Disputes of 1924. This was an ingenious plan to link security and disarmament *and* compulsory arbitration to determine the aggressor in disputed cases, but, by the time it reached its final form, the Protocol was so freighted with loopholes and reservations that it would be virtually inoperable.[9] Still the Dominions objected and the Conservatives campaigned against the Protocol in the 1924 election. Thus, Britain rejected the Geneva Protocol in March 1925.

With the failure of two efforts by the League to bolster the peace, European diplomats fell back on the more traditional approach of defensive alliances. As Germany faced the prospect of a network of alliances against her she reacted and, as a result, a west European security pact gradually emerged. Although envisaged by some as a means to reinforce the peace, it was intended by others as a device to revise the peace settlement. On balance it did the latter, as a plan initially intended to enhance French security and thus pave the way for pacification redounded to the advantage of Germany and to the detriment of France and her east-European allies.

The 1924 reparations settlement had defused a major issue and thus, in a sense, it paved the way for further pacification. On the other hand it had intensified French fears as Frenchmen looked across the Rhine and saw a larger, more populous, industrially stronger Germany rapidly returning to economic health and prosperity. When the new Conservative government in London quickly noted the brooding concern over security in Paris, the francophile Chamberlain determined to allay French fears by an Anglo-Belgian-French security system. However, his policy was soon turned to another path toward peace by Stresemann, substantially abetted by the British ambassador in Berlin, Lord D'Abernon.

Stresemann of course did not welcome the prospect of an Anglo-French-Belgian combination against Germany tied through France to Poland in the east and Czechoslovakia to the south. Further, while he had laid the reparations issue to rest for the time being, he had not solved the disarmament question which threatened to delay the scheduled evacuation of the first (Cologne) Rhineland zone on 1 January 1925. Under the Versailles Treaty the Rhineland was to be evacuated in three stages in 1925, 1930 and 1935, but the occupation could be prolonged indefinitely if Germany had not fulfilled her obligations. Several specific grounds existed but, with the reparations settlement, the issue had narrowed to disarmament. The Inter-Allied Military Control Commission (I.M.C.C.), which had been unsuccessfully attempting to supervise German disarmament to treaty levels, had been withdrawn during the Ruhr occupation since the German government refused to guarantee the safety of its members. However, in August 1924 Herriot, partly as the price for French agreement to the London reparations settlement, prevailed upon MacDonald to join in telling Germany that the Cologne zone would not be evacuated until the I.M.C.C. had returned to Germany to establish whether she had honoured her disarmament obligations. It was understood that this would be a final investigation by the I.M.C.C. and that, upon Entente satisfaction, Cologne would be evacuated and further supervision of German disarmament would be transferred to the League, whose inspections (as Germany hoped and France feared) would probably be ephemeral.

After considerable foot-dragging, Stresemann conceded and the I.M.C.C. returned to Germany. It was unable to complete its labours by 1 January 1925, but in December 1924 issued an interim report indicating large-scale German default on most military clauses of the Versailles Treaty. Accordingly Germany was notified that the Cologne zone would not be evacuated on schedule. Thus Stresemann faced the problem of achieving evacuation without disarmament. His solution, to submerge the issue in a Rhineland pact, was highly successful. By the time the I.M.C.C.'s Final Report of 15 February 1925 announced Germany's failure to disarm in 160 pages of damning detail,[10] the negotiations toward the Locarno treaties were under way. While satisfaction was requested (but not always obtained) on a few key points, the I.M.C.C. report largely fell by the wayside. German failure to disarm did not become a major issue because such an issue could jeopardise the Rhineland pact, which was clearly tied to evacuation of the Cologne zone and a reduction of the occupation in the remaining Rhineland zones. The juridical link between disarmament and evacuation was direct; there was no legal connection whatever between evacuation and the Locarno treaties, but it was universally understood that evacuation was the price Stresemann demanded for the Rhineland pact he offered.

His first overture to Chamberlain in January 1925, essentially a revival of the plan proposed in December 1922 in an effort to prevent the Ruhr occupation, made the connection clear. Stresemann had been prodded to his offer by D'Abernon, who was operating outside his instructions and contrary to Chamberlain's policy of Anglo-French entente. Stresemann, however, assumed that the initiative had British blessing and approached London.[11] Apart from informing Paris and urging Germany to do the same, Chamberlain took little action at first. Until early March both he and the Cabinet were torn by political manoeuvring, consideration of the Geneva Protocol, fear of French military might (especially French air-power), desire to link Britain to France's army, which was the largest on the continent, and interest in the German offer. In Paris Herriot, whose hopes rested on the Geneva Protocol, also took no action. But in early March Chamberlain saw him to break the news that Britain would reject the Protocol and had decided that the German offer provided an appropriate route to peace and security.

There ensued a hiatus until May while France and Belgium had general elections, the British Foreign Office reorganised itself after the sudden death of the permanent under-secretary, Sir Eyre Crowe, and Germany elected Field Marshal Paul von Hindenburg to fill the vacancy created by the death of President Friedrich Ebert. Although Hindenburg's past had been ultra-conservative, monarchist and militarist, Stresemann assured nervous western diplomatists that his accession would only bring right-wing support to the government's policy of detente. The election to the German presidency of the pre-eminent symbol of the Kaiser's militarism was not allowed to disrupt negotiations, so greatly was the advent of true peace desired.

When negotiations resumed in May, the men of Locarno were all in place. Foremost among these were Briand, Chamberlain and Stresemann. These three controlled their respective countries' foreign policies until 1929 (and Briand until 1932). Collectively they were awarded the 1926 Nobel Peace Prize for their labours at Locarno in 1925, and collectively they dominated European diplomacy for the remainder of the twenties. They became very well acquainted, but in 1925 they were taking each other's measure for the first time.

Of the three Stresemann had been in power the longest. When he took office in 1923 and called off the Ruhr resistance, Stresemann enunciated a policy of fulfilment of the Versailles Treaty. Few, even in Germany, recognised that the object of 'fulfilment' was to dismantle the treaty as rapidly as possible. Stresemann substituted conciliation for truculence to achieve a goal which had never changed. It is often said that a diplomatist must lie for his country and Stresemann was a superlative liar, dispensing total untruths to the Entente, the German people, and his diary with even-handed aplomb.[12] He had substantial political difficulties, as the German left distrusted his conservative past and the German right thought he was conceding too much to the Entente; Stresemann made the most of these to gain foreign concessions. Entente leaders, anxious to keep in office this 'good European' (who was in fact a great German nationalist), generally gave way. Stresemann invariably had a list of concessions to Germany necessary to achieve the pacification of Europe. As he achieved one concession from the top of the list, two or three more were always added at the bottom. Stresemann gained most of his list, and no man in the Weimar Republic did more to destroy the Versailles Treaty. Unfortunately, his last great achievement, the full evacuation of the Rhineland five years ahead of schedule in 1930 (after his death but his achievement none the less), burst the bonds of pent-up German nationalism and paved the way for Hitler.[13]

Stresemann's adversary was Briand. Much the most flexible of French Foreign Ministers and much the most of a 'good European', he dominated French foreign policy through successive coalition Cabinets, as did his counterpart across the Rhine. Briand was often accused, especially by the old men of the French right, of being naive and easily duped by Stresemann. However, the perceptive Briand well recognised that he had inherited a situation wherein France had already played her last trump and had not won. As Stresemann wanted to keep Briand in office, Briand pleaded his own political difficulties to forestall concessions, but with less success than Stresemann since France became increasingly isolated whenever she attempted to enforce any part of the Versailles Treaty. Briand soon recognised Stresemann's goals and saw that they would be achieved, given the international climate of opinion. Thus he sought to impose new bonds on Germany through European economic and diplomatic integration. Briand became a leading advocate of all forms of European union in an effort to enmesh Germany so deeply in all-European economic, political, and diplomatic arrangements that she could never make war on France again. Since all the old sanctions were gone, this seemed the only route remaining toward French security. Briand pursued it with energy as the alternative was too frightful to contemplate.[14]

If D'Abernon was perhaps the true father of the Locarno settlement, Chamberlain was undoubtedly its midwife. Through the spring, summer and autumn of 1925 he persevered, although often infuriated by Stresemann's increasing demands. In the end he brought France and Germany warily together. Locarno was his triumph and he exulted in it. He was also the one true believer at Locarno, thinking he had indeed achieved genuine peace.[15] He did not at first see that he had achieved an extraordinary improvement in Britain's power position, making her the arbiter of European peace, for such was not his goal. Chamberlain considered Locarno the peak of his career, and thus developed a great fondness for all the men of Locarno except Vandervelde. He was particularly grateful to Mussolini for his participation. This attitude led him in later years to be more indulgent of Italian escapades than he might otherwise have been.

The other two men of Locarno were the Fascist Mussolini and the socialist Vandervelde, whose 1925 tenure at the Belgian Foreign Ministry brought the security arrangements so long sought by his Liberal and Catholic predecessors, Paul Hymans and Henri Jaspar. This was an accident of timing and Vandervelde had little to say

about the Locarno arrangements. He also had nothing to say to
Mussolini, to whom he was not speaking as a result of incidents in
their mutual socialist past and Mussolini's Fascist present, notably
the recent murder of the Italian socialist Giacomo Matteotti.[16]
Mussolini also had little to say about the Locarno arrangements,
thanks to his own vacillation. When first asked if Italy would join
Britain in guaranteeing German treaties with France and Belgium
reaffirming the Rhineland frontiers, Mussolini angled for a guarantee of the Brenner frontier between Italy and Austria. Stresemann
replied that such would be possible only if *Anschluss* were permitted,
for Germany was not at present on the Brenner Pass, and that
ended that.[17] Thereafter Mussolini showed only intermittent
interest, torn between his desire to avoid commitments north of the
Alps and his equal desire to seize the opportunity for glory inherent
in joining with Britain to guarantee the peace of Europe. Much
disliking international conferences where he had to share the limelight, he half hoped that no treaties would materialise and so stayed
away from the Locarno meetings at first. When it became clear that
success was in sight he roared up Lake Maggiore in a speedboat,
arrived with his usual noisy panache, and signed the agreements.[18]

There perhaps should have been two or three other men of
Locarno. Stresemann's original offer provided only for a mutual
guarantee of the permanence of the Franco-German frontier and
the demilitarised zone in the Rhineland. Entente pressure extended
the guarantee to the Belgian border and there was talk of a
guarantee of Germany's other frontiers with Austria, Czechoslovakia
and Poland. Austria was soon dropped, but Chamberlain made one
effort and Briand several to extract a reaffirmation of the Polish and
Czech frontiers from Stresemann, who said he could not guarantee
these borders in perpetuity and could only promise that they would
not be altered by force (although frontiers are rarely altered in any
other way). In the end he would not even put this promise in
writing. As Britain decided that her efforts to keep the peace could
go to the Rhine but not to the Vistula, Briand had to concede and
content himself with finding a way to reaffirm France's guarantee
of Poland and Czechoslovakia, embodied in alliances with both
countries. Even that proved difficult and had to be done indirectly.
The Polish Foreign Minister of the moment, Count Alexandre
Skrzyński, and the perennial Czech Foreign Minister, Édouard

Beneš, who dominated interwar Czech foreign policy, were allowed to attend the closing days of the Locarno conference to collect the few small crumbs allotted to them but, as Stresemann accurately and openly boasted, 'Herren Beneš and Skrzyński had to sit in a neighbouring room until we let them in. Such was the situation of the states which had been so pampered until then, because they were the servants of the others, but were dropped the moment there seemed a prospect of coming to an understanding with Germany.'[19]

Before the men of Locarno could gather in that small Swiss town to rearrange the peace of Europe, there was much negotiating to be done. It was carried out through normal diplomatic channels during the summer of 1925.[20] The shape of things to come soon became clear. Germany on the one hand and France and Belgium on the other would mutually forswear war against each other and reaffirm both the absolute permanence of their existing frontiers and the inviolability of the Rhineland demilitarised zone, while Britain and perhaps Italy would guarantee these pledges, committed to aid against any violator of them.

It was also soon clear that Germany must enter the League of Nations as part of the agreement. Stresemann wanted to join the League (and had in fact applied for membership in 1924) but also wanted to extract maximum concessions for doing so. Pointing to German hostility to anything connected with the Versailles Treaty, he indicated that Germany must be given back all her pre-war colonies, a permanent seat of the League Council, and full exemption from Article 16 of the League Covenant calling for sanctions against aggressors (on account of Germany's exposed geographic position and alleged disarmament). The colonies were a bargaining counter and Stresemann gained the rest. Whenever negotiations became sticky, he would murmur that Germany would never undertake sanctions against Russia,[21] thus raising the spectre of greater Russo-German rapprochement to scare the Entente into concessions.

It was agreed as well that the Rhineland pact should be tied to the League and that the League Council should determine violations of the treaties, but there was much difficulty over mechanics. Britain insisted that there should be no obligation to act until the Council had declared a violation. Given French, British, Italian and German permanent seats on the Council and the unanimity requirement, such a proviso could have rendered the guarantee a nullity. French protests led to a distinction between violations and 'flagrant military violations' involving troop movements across frontiers or into the demilitarised zone, which required immediate aid in advance of Council deliberations.

With this the scheme moved toward achievement. Neither Stresemann's demands nor a strident German denunciation of the 'war guilt clause' deflected the course of events. At the start of September a meeting in London of German and Entente jurists, somewhat delayed by an unexpected Italian decision to send an observer, ironed out many details.[22] After a pause while all the Foreign Ministers except Stresemann attended the annual League Assembly meetings at Geneva in September, the statesmen gathered on 5 October at Locarno in southern Switzerland to solemnise what they had arranged. Locarno had been chosen by Stresemann as a neutral site, a small town with fewer gawking bystanders than a large city, and a location convenient for Mussolini should he decide to come.

The prevailing ambiance at Locarno was public amiability. There were smiling strolls through town, a cosy chat between Briand and the German Chancellor Hans Luther in a nearby *albergo*, a famous boating expedition on Lake Maggiore, and a distinctly hilarious press luncheon where Entente and German leaders broke bread together for the first time.[23] All this was a far cry from the grim tension of earlier international conferences with Germany. It was noteworthy that there was no Entente gathering prior to Locarno and that, at Locarno itself, private Entente sessions were few. Clearly Stresemann had brought Germany a long way on the road to diplomatic respectability and had done much to weaken the western Entente.

Behind the scenes hard and often bitter bargaining continued as he tried to extract further concessions. On the boating excursion, sea, sun and champagne yielded the '*texte de bateau*', which essentially promised that Germany would be exempted from the Covenant Article 16 obligation to engage in sanctions, either economic or military, against aggressors. The wording, declaring that each League member should 'resist every act of aggression in a measure compatible with its military situation and which takes account of its geographic position'[24] suggested that each country could decide for itself whether it had any obligation to participate in any agreed sanctions, but only Vandervelde displayed concern about the implications for the future of the League and he was overridden.

The five-hour trip of the good ship *Orange Blossom* also yielded a second German triumph. France abandoned any explicit guarantee of the arbitration treaties to be signed between Germany and both Poland and Czechoslovakia, although retaining an implicit right to come to their aid in case of attack. Thereafter progress was swift and the treaties soon took shape. Within a few days Stresemann demanded virtual cancellation of the Versailles Treaty including drastic changes in the Rhineland as the advance price of German ratification. He got nothing except what he wanted most: a French promise that once agreement was reached on disarmament and a start made, Germany's word would be taken about execution without inspection and the Cologne zone would be evacuated. By this time Briand was entirely committed to the pact and prepared to give Stresemann what he needed to ensure its approval. Besides, with a sickly franc he could not alienate the Anglo-American financial community, and he could not afford to fail once more to gain the British guarantee of France, even in an inferior form.

Stresemann continued to angle for further concessions while the jurists tied up loose ends and the statesmen solved a thorny question. They all wanted to append their names to the historic documents being prepared, but none had full powers to sign. Thus they decided to initial the treaties of Locarno *at* Locarno, and Chamberlain invited them all to London for a signing ceremony later. The British delegation had conspired to ensure that the closing ceremonies at Locarno would fall upon 16 October, Chamberlain's sixty-second birthday. So the men of Locarno gathered for the last time that Friday evening at the little mairie of Locarno, initialed their pacts, and spoke their speeches. Then they came forth on the balcony to show the historic treaties to the crowds gathered in the dusk. Briand bussed Luther on the cheek; old women knelt in the dust to cross themselves; church bells rang out over the lake; fireworks erupted in the evening sky; and the normally staid citizens of Locarno celebrated the advent of peace until daybreak.[25]

Chamberlain's birthday present came in several packages. Germany signed arbitration treaties with France, Belgium, Poland and Czechoslovakia, while France signed new treaties of mutual assistance with Poland and Czechoslovakia to compensate for the absence of any German guarantee of the eastern frontiers. Above all the five-power Rhineland Pact guaranteed the maintenance of the existing Belgo-German and Franco-German frontiers and the demilitarised zone, committed Britain and Italy to act against any violation of this territorial *status quo*, and provided for arbitration to resolve future disputes. The Rhineland powers forswore war with each other except in narrowly defined circumstances which would permit France to aid Poland in the event of German attack. Violations of this treaty, which would enter into force when Germany joined the League, would be referred to the League Council and elaborate procedures were provided both for its actions and for arbitration of disputes to avoid violations and war.[26] The clear intent of the Locarno treaties was to freeze the Rhineland frontiers in perpetuity in order to remove a major impediment to permanent peace. Treaties, however, may be read in many ways. Within a few days of the ceremony at Locarno Stresemann unsuccessfully sought retrocession of Eupen and Malmédy from Belgium, claiming that he had only promised not to alter the frontier by military means.[27]

Since on that October evening the treaties of Locarno gained an instant sanctity normally accorded only to motherhood and no politician in power dared speak against them, it is hard to know what the men of Locarno really thought of what they had wrought. Mussolini was clearly unhappy, having gained a commitment he did not want and nothing that he did want. Chamberlain was euphoric. Like the people of Locarno and most ordinary Europeans, he thought he had made peace. Stresemann, while not euphoric by nature, knew he had gained a great victory with more to come. He had restored Germany to equality and diplomatic respectability, dissolved the disarmament deadlock, forestalled an Entente alliance against Germany and weakened the Entente in the guise of a greater detente with Germany, resolved the Rhineland evacuation (for he would not enter the League and bring the treaties into force until Cologne was evacuated), conceded almost nothing, and gained much. More could be gained as the price of German ratification and League entry, and surely the spirit of Locarno would yield opportunities for further treaty revision. Stresemann well knew that all was now possible as the price of fulfilment so long as he did not send troops across a western frontier or into the demilitarised zone. The implications did not escape French and Belgian leaders; privately they were pessimistic, but the long-sought British guarantee had to be taken in the only form in which it was offered and there was naught to do but accept the changed situation. Polish and Czech leaders also had no choice but to accept, but they did so in fear. As leading beneficiaries of the Paris settlement, they had wanted to see it preserved, not undermined, and they knew they were the losers of Locarno.[28]

In negotiating the Rhineland pact, Germany made much of the fact that she was now offering voluntarily to affirm what had been imposed upon her by *force majeure* in the Versailles Treaty. Stresemann emphasised that the voluntary affirmation was considerably more binding than the Versailles *diktat*. Chamberlain so badly wanted peace, while France and Belgium so deeply craved security that the argument was accepted. However, reaffirmation of some treaty clauses not only implied a need for such action but also cast doubt on the validity and binding force of others. Stresemann intended this effect regarding the Polish frontier which he flatly refused to mention in the treaties. Locarno was widely interpreted as a green light for Germany in the east. Well before the treaties were completed, a German diplomatist remarked, 'I am a poor German but I would not wish to be Polish, for there would not pass a night when I would sleep tranquilly.'[29]

Even in the west much had changed. The French troops had left the Ruhr and could never return, for if they did Britain and Italy must go to Germany's aid. France could not even seize customs revenues without facing, at a minimum, a ruling from the League Council (in which the veto was now abandoned by interested parties in disputes arising out of the Locarno pacts), probably in support of Germany. France's powers of enforcement were gone and, while the Locarno treaties nominally strengthened the League by giving it supervision of execution, in fact the reinterpretation of Article 16 meant that the League had lost what little power of enforcement it had ever possessed. To gain this pact so unfavourable to France and her allies, Briand had promised to end the disarmament dispute without further ado, to release German prisoners held by France and Belgium on charges stemming from both the war and the Ruhr occupation, to evacuate Cologne shortly, and to reduce the occupation in the two remaining zones. The instruments of coercion embodied in the Versailles Treaty had all but disappeared. In fact Germany could default with impunity if she chose

Locarno Pacts 1925

on disarmament and reparations, France's two greatest concerns, and France would be helpless to act.

Briand had accepted this situation partly to get the British guarantee and partly because the diplomatic isolation stemming from the Ruhr occupation and the continuing weakness of the franc made any policy contrary to Anglo-American diplomatic and financial interests impossible. Briand knew that France's position was fundamentally untenable and that the alteration of the power balance implicit in Locarno had become inevitable. He was trying to salvage what he could, and the British guarantee was his consolation prize. However, it was an illusory guarantee.

The Locarno guarantees were from the start inoperable. The British quickly realised that having guaranteed both sides of the Rhenish frontier they must make military arrangements with all three countries or with none, so they made them with none.[30] Given the speed and complexity of modern military operations, a guarantee of immediate action against flagrant military violations without detailed technical preparations was a nullity; a country could easily be engulfed before help arrived.[31] Further, the British army was small and much of it was stationed in Palestine, India, and the other outer reaches of Empire. What was left available to Europe was militarily laughable.

Yet Locarno made Britain the arbiter of Europe's peace and restored her to her favourite position as the balance in the balance of power, able not only to tip it against the evil-doer but in large part to determine who the evil-doer might be. In the meantime her hands were free. It seems incongruous that a largely disarmed Britain became the primary instrument for the enforcement of peace. Yet Briand and Stresemann both knew that, should another Franco-German collision be protracted, the British navy, the British Empire, and the British ties to the American financial community might again be decisive. In the long run, as the Versailles Treaty was further dismantled, the power balance would tip increasingly toward Germany, but for the moment Britain held the balance. Neither Briand nor Stresemann seriously considered crossing the Rhineland frontier.

The Rhineland pact was unpopular in Germany precisely because it guaranteed the western frontier and thus precluded reversion to the 1914 boundaries, which most Germans still considered their birthright. Stresemann could not enunciate the extent of his triumph to the German electorate without creating acute political difficulties for the other men of Locarno, especially Briand, whom he wished to keep at the Quai d'Orsay. Consequently Stresemann used his own political difficulties to extract further concessions as the price of German ratification. Most of what he gained had been foreshadowed at Locarno itself. Germany's word that such disarmament as was being required had been carried out was accepted with unseemly haste and I.M.C.C. representatives were instructed not to haggle over details. The Entente powers publicly announced that evacuation at Cologne would commence on 1 December, the date scheduled for the London signing ceremonies of the Locarno treaties, and later indicated that evacuation would probably be completed by 31 January 1926, as indeed it was. The Entente further promised to reduce the I.M.C.C. to a token level, to overlook German police quartered in barracks (a substantial, seasoned military force outside the limits imposed by the Versailles Treaty), to reduce the size of the Rhineland occupation and to make a long list of changes there, all ardently desired by Germany and all tending to give the occupation a less permanent and more temporary character. With that, the Reichstag approved the treaties of Locarno.[32]

Yet still Stresemann sent word that he wished to talk business when he came to London for the signing ceremonies. For the first time a German move did not evoke any Entente consultation at all, not even through ordinary diplomatic channels. There was almost no discussion among Paris, London and Brussels. It was already evident that as the Versailles Treaty was progressively dismantled, there would in future be fewer occasions when Germany would ask and the Entente would be obliged to answer in unison. But the absence of Entente consultation before the London meeting raised the larger question of the future of the Entente. It had come into being as a result of the war and its function was to enforce the peace, particularly in regard to Germany. Yet it had abandoned this task and was now seeking peace through detente with Germany. If this detente became actual, the Entente would lose its raison d'être and cease to exist.

At London detente was less than total. After the public signing ceremonies on 1 December 1925 and speeches hailing both peace and the spirit of Locarno which would make peace real at last the men of Locarno met privately once more. Stresemann demanded and got further troop reductions in the remaining Rhineland zones and an end to billeting on the population there. He complained that the I.M.C.C. was 'over-punctilious' and, while he did not obtain full withdrawal of the I.M.C.C., he did gain further reduction to two small detachments. He obtained other concessions as well, but Briand indicated that more changes were not possible overnight and Chamberlain was emphatic that the colonies would not be returned.[33] As usual, Stresemann went home with most but not all of his lengthening list accomplished or developing nicely.

As the year turned and the Entente troops came home from Cologne, Europe celebrated the advent of true peace. Henceforth the spirit of Locarno would reign, substituting conciliation for enforcement as the basis for peace. Yet for some peace remained a desperate hope rather than an actuality. A few men knew that the spirit of Locarno was a fragile foundation on which to build a lasting peace. After all, the real spirit at Locarno behind the façade of public fellowship was one of bitter confrontation between a fearful France flanked by the unhappy east Europeans, trying to hide their humiliation and panic, and a resentful, revisionist Germany demanding ever more alterations in the power balance to her benefit. Since Germany was potentially the strongest power on the continent, the private fears of her neighbours could only deepen.

Yet the public faces remained serene and smiling, and the ordinary European did not know about the clashes behind closed doors. He knew only that Germans and Frenchmen had gone boating together and had chatted of peace at a small inn. The public façade of the Locarno conference and the treaties themselves had created an illusion of peace, and ordinary men rejoiced. Misled by a false front Europe thankfully entered upon the Locarno years, thinking that real peace had arrived at last. Of all the interwar years these were perhaps the best years, but none the less they were years of illusion.

detente is used in correct translational form

4 The Years of Illusion

BEFORE the euphoria engendered by the Locarno meetings had time to fade another episode heightened the illusion that peace had finally arrived and that henceforth conciliation would reign. Scarcely a week after the triumphant conclusion at Locarno skirmishes on the Greco-Bulgarian frontier erupted into a Greek military invasion of Bulgaria, who appealed at once to the League of Nations. The events which ensued gave the League a much-needed but illusory success.

Briand, to whom the rotating presidency of the Council had fallen, convoked an emergency session and despatched an immediate telegram to both countries calling for an end to hostilities and withdrawal of forces. As a consequence a further Greek offensive was cancelled but skirmishes continued. Under Briand's firm leadership the Council refused to hear arguments on the issue until each army was behind its own frontier. As the great powers made concerted démarches in Athens, sent observers to the area, and threatened both naval demonstrations and sanctions under Article 16 of the Covenant, the Greeks withdrew. Thereafter the League investigated the episode, established responsibility (finding some Bulgar provocation) and levied an indemnity, which Greece paid. It appeared that pacific settlement of international disputes was a reality.[1] Actually the successful resolution of the Greco-Bulgarian clash arose from a rare unanimity among the European major powers, energetic action on their part including threats of force, the internal weakness of the Greek regime which made the bluff easy to call, and the important fact that the parties to the dispute were small states susceptible to great-power pressure. What had occurred was an almost Metternichean manoeuvre reminiscent of the early nineteenth-century Concert of Europe so heartily condemned by proponents of the League.

There was much rejoicing, self-congratulation, and optimism about the growing importance and success of the League at the

December Council meeting where the Greco-Bulgarian dispute was settled. While this satisfaction was misguided and self-delusive, those few months after Locarno were perhaps the League's brief heyday, the one moment when the League's future seemed bright. It had halted a shooting war (or appeared to have done so) and had precariously managed to delimit the disputed Turko-Iraqi boundary despite the involvement of Britain as mandatory power in Iraq. By this time the League Council met quarterly in regularly scheduled sessions which most European Foreign Ministers attended, thus turning the spotlight onto Geneva. Further, the greatest threat to European tranquillity, the tension between France and Germany, appeared misleadingly to have been entombed at Locarno, and Germany's entry into the League was anticipated in the new year. There was no expectation that either America or Russia would join in the foreseeable future, but at last all other powers of consequence would belong. The League's proponents predicted that henceforth its role in European matters would be enlarged, with decisions made in the League halls at Geneva, not by the treaty agencies in Paris or the Entente powers in conference. Few foresaw that German entry into the League would transform it, while the activities of the Locarno powers would undermine it. Most hailed Locarno heartily and awaited German entry eagerly. However, by February 1926, when the German application arrived, it was becoming clear that such optimism was premature, while the unseemly squabble which ensued demonstrated openly that brotherly love did not yet reign at Geneva.

Since the Locarno treaties would not take effect until Germany entered the League, her application was anticipated and careful preparations had been made in Berlin and Geneva. These preparations had overlooked one problem, however. Under Article 4 of the Covenant, there was no way to grant Germany the permanent Council seat demanded in her earlier 1924 application (without objection from other members) and clearly promised to her at Locarno without opening up the larger question of the composition of the Council in general. There was no disagreement about either Germany's admission or her claim to a permanent Council seat, but German entry was jeopardised and delayed by the heated controversy caused by the additional claims of existing members.

Some of these claims were of long standing, and the difficulty should have been foreseen. Tension over the composition of the Council had been rising for several years, and the German application merely provided an opportunity for it to erupt. The claims of Spain to represent the Hispanic powers and of Brazil to represent the Americas in the absence of the United States, both with permanent seats, had been seriously discussed at Geneva in 1921 and 1923. For several years China had argued for both a geographic distribution of seats and her own claim to great-power status. Poland's claim, the most explosive politically, was the most recent but had been foreshadowed from the moment that German entry was seriously considered, on the grounds that Germany could be expected to use her Council seat to press for treaty revision at Poland's expense. Yet at Locarno the clear understanding had been that Germany alone would be granted a permanent seat in recognition of her undoubted great-power status. In his insistence that this implicit promise be honoured without modification, Stresemann was on solid footing.

When Germany's application for membership arrived in Geneva, Brazil, Poland and Spain filed claims for permanent seats on the Council, thus forcing the issue of its composition. China (and later Persia) filed a contingency claim that, *if* the number of permanent seats were increased, she should have one. These claims reflected growing dissatisfaction with European domination of the Council, an increasing tendency toward informal regional groupings to gain regional representation, and the emergence of intermediate powers. The Covenant distinguished only between great powers with permanent Council seats and small powers eligible to compete for temporary seats. Yet even a weak China torn by civil strife clearly outranked Siam, Brazil obviously overshadowed El Salvador, and Poland was more powerful than Latvia.

The claims of the intermediate powers met with little enthusiasm. They created a problem that diplomatists preferred to avoid, which perhaps explains in part why nothing was settled before the League Assembly met. Secondly, as a contemporary British observer remarked:

From the West-European point of view it seemed intolerable that the destinies of a region which was the cultural center of the Western World should be at the mercy of outlying countries whose international position was comparatively secure and whose contributions to the common culture of Western society could hardly be compared to those of France, Germany, and Great Britain.[2]

Further, the European great powers, with the customary arrogance of great powers, assumed that they should settle the matter themselves, preferably in a private gathering of the Locarno signatories. Finally, the smaller European states, led by Sweden, announced sharp opposition to any enlargement of the number of permanent seats beyond that for Germany. Sweden, Denmark, Belgium, and other less vocal European members had a clear stake in the pacification of Europe implicit in rapid German entry, disliked any dilution of the European representation on the Council, and were alert to the threat to themselves in any distinction between small and intermediate powers. Thus they vociferously backed the great-power inclination to resist the new claims, which were pressed with increasing publicity in advance of the Assembly meeting.

On 8 March 1926 the special session of the Assembly called for the express purpose of German admission convened without any solution in sight. Since Stresemann and Luther had arrived in a special train crammed with diplomatists and documents,[3] some were hopeful that the problem would soon be solved. Disillusionment came swiftly. As the technicalities attendant on German entry were trivial, they were completed quickly. Thereafter the delegates sat idle in humiliating ignorance while the Locarno powers tried to arrange matters behind closed doors.

Pressures on the three principal claimants were initially unavailing while Sweden reiterated opposition to any enlargement of the Council beyond Germany, whether by permanent or non-permanent seats. Despite that, an attempt was made to resolve matters by awarding a permanent place to Germany and creating an additional non-permanent seat for Poland, but Germany rejected this scheme. Finally, in a move which was less altruistic than it appeared to be, Sweden offered to vacate her present seat in favour of Poland.[4] Stresemann agreed, provided that Czechoslovakia would also vacate in favour of Holland in order to reduce the pro-French cast of the Council. But Brazil balked. Since she indicated her intention (as occupant of a temporary seat) to veto Germany's permanent place on the Council unless she also received one, there was naught to do but refer the matter to a committee and postpone German entry. At the final Assembly session to approve these arrangements the Netherlands and Norway bitterly denounced the closed-door gatherings (which were already known as 'Locarno tea parties') and the damage being done to the League's structure of committees, which remained unused throughout the special session.

Fortunately German nationalists reacted to the delay by concluding that since Council seats were so hard to get and so widely desired they must be more valuable than hitherto supposed. Thus Stresemann's political difficulties were diminished, not increased. Still, he made the most of the opportunity. On 24 April 1926 in Berlin, he signed a treaty of neutrality and non-aggression with Russia to reinforce the treaty of Rapallo. This pact, which had been negotiated concurrently with that of Locarno, was designed to quiet Russian apprehensions about the Locarno alignment, maintain the Russian connection, appease the russophile element within Germany, counter-balance Locarno, and encourage Entente concessions. While the text of the Treaty of Berlin was innocuous,[5] France and the east-European allies were alarmed. Moreover Stresemann claimed that Hindenburg was objecting to League entry and that three conditions would be necessary to pacify the 'Old Gentleman': (1) a sharp reduction in the number of occupation troops, (2) an agreement on the duration of the Rhineland occupation, thus implying early evacuation, and (3) an end to the work of the I.M.C.C. As usual Stresemann sought additional concessions as Germany's reward for accepting concessions already gained. But this time Chamberlain, who had defended the Russo-German treaty, sharply told Stresemann not to bargain.[6] None the less, the special Committee on the Composition of the Council renewed its efforts.

In the late summer it arrived at a solution of sorts. Germany alone would gain a permanent place, but the number of non-permanent seats would be increased from six to nine. Of these, six or more would carry three-year non-renewable terms, creating a long-desired rotation system, but a maximum of three intended for Brazil, Poland and Spain could be specified as eligible for re-election, thus creating a class of semi-permanent seats for some of the intermediate powers. Poland accepted this scheme, but Brazil and Spain declared their intention to withdraw from the League. Before the mandatory two-year period of notice expired Spain returned to Geneva, but Brazil did not, becoming the first state to leave the League (except for Costa Rica, who could not meet the annual assessments). Poland took her semi-permanent seat, and there soon developed an informal understanding about geographic allocation of the other eight temporary seats. Thus European domination of the Council became somewhat less obvious but, as European dominance of the League itself in fact increased, the non-European states were left with the illusion of power, not the reality.

Nobody much liked the solution arrived at by the committee on the composition of the Council but, as there was no other, everybody except Brazil and Spain accepted it in order to facilitate German entry into the League. That long-heralded event took place during the regular annual Assembly session. It was a grand occasion, only somewhat dampened by the thunderous squall which had gone before. On 10 September 1926, the twelfth anniversary of the battle of the Marne, the German delegation formally entered the Assembly Hall at Geneva and Stresemann accepted membership in an address with only muted revisionist and nationalist overtones. Briand, chosen to speak alone for the League as Europe's greatest orator and as the leading apostle of Franco-German conciliation, replied in a soaring oration assuring the world that the long history of bloody Franco-German conflict had ended. To delirious applause, he cried, 'Away with rifles, machine guns, and cannon! Make way for conciliation, arbitration and peace!'[7] The spirit of Locarno appeared to have triumphed.

In a sense it had, although not as the smaller states had hoped. To their delight Briand's speech had deplored the secret diplomacy of the special session. But his actions soon belied his words. A week later came the famous interview at Thoiry, a secret luncheon meeting between Stresemann and Briand, the first of their private sessions together. At first Thoiry was regarded as an omen of conciliation, but in time such meetings evoked increasing dismay, especially since the Locarno tea-parties at Geneva continued unabated, despite cries of secret diplomacy from the excluded smaller states.

One effect of Locarno and the concomitant German entry into the League was that Germany, the leading revisionist state, was admitted to a position of power in an organisation largely designed to uphold the *status quo*. Inevitably the smaller European states most dedicated to maintenance of the *status quo* took alarm, especially since at Thoiry Stresemann once again sought retrocession of Eupen and Malmédy. Another effect of full German diplomatic rehabilitation was that Germany was now admitted to the hotel-room diplomacy of Geneva, and inevitably that diplomacy changed, signalling a significant shift in the balance of power and an alteration in the character of Geneva's closed-door deliberations. While in the past hotel-room negotiations had served for the quiet resolution of disputes between two countries and for regional caucuses of the smaller states, such as the Little Entente and the Latin American bloc, the Locarno tea-parties had a very different character, extending to the full range of European problems and sometimes beyond. Meanwhile the agenda of the League was reduced to trivia. A League official later remarked that the Council 'listened to brilliant but interminable speeches on the claims of Hungarian landowners to be compensated by the Roumanian government for their properties distributed among the peasants of Transylvania. But of the greatest questions it heard nothing.'[8]

These questions were settled in the hotel rooms of the Locarno powers, who continued the *politique des casinos* at Geneva, thus obviating the need for formal international conferences to settle the leading issues of the day. Sometimes these issues properly fell under the Locarno pacts although, even so, Poland and Czechoslovakia were excluded. Often they did not. In 1927, when Italy accused Yugoslavia of preparing an invasion of Albania, Mussolini prevailed upon Chamberlain and Briand to block a Yugoslav appeal to the Council, and the matter was discussed only in a Locarno party without Yugoslav participation.[9] Such episodes evoked constant protest from small states but to little avail. The most conspicuous figures of Geneva, such as Beneš of Czechoslovakia, Hymans of Belgium, Fridtjof Nansen of Norway, Östen Undén of Sweden, and Guiseppe Motta of Switzerland, found themselves helpless in the face of the reality of great-power politics.

When the composition of the League Council was originally debated in 1919 in terms of great-power representation only, Paul Hymans had shouted, 'What you propose is a revival of the Holy Alliance of unhallowed memory!'[10] Now it had revived in another form, less official but equally forceful. And Stresemann was surely the Talleyrand of this twentieth-century alliance. As the nineteenth-century Concert against France had rapidly been converted into a Quintuple Alliance including France, so the Entente against Germany had welcomed Stresemann to its hotel-room deliberations. While Belgian and Japanese representatives were usually in attendance, the Locarno tea-parties in fact constituted a Concert of the four great European powers although, given Mussolini's lack of enthusiasm for both Locarno and the League, more often the new Quadruple Alliance was reduced to the Locarno triumvirate of Britain, France and Germany.

This arrangement derived in part from the natural arrogance of great powers and their inevitable tendency to reserve decisions to themselves. In part it derived from Stresemann's conviction that rapid revision of the peace settlement could best be achieved through personal cultivation of Briand and from Briand's preference to perform his foot-dragging in private, not in public. Then, too, Chamberlain had a great fondness for France in general and for Briand in particular. He regarded Locarno as his finest achievement and displayed a natural tendency to prolong its rosy glow. He emphatically wished to limit British commitments and considered Locarno that limit. Thus Chamberlain preferred Locarno tea-parties to League assemblies, even referring revealingly at Geneva to 'your Council' and 'your Assembly'.[11] He was more than pleased to escape from the universal commitments embodied in League membership into cosy meetings of the European Concert he had created at Locarno.

The nineteenth-century Metternichean Concert of Europe quickly foundered on the hard rock of diverging interests of the great powers. The same problem soon caused the Locarno triumvirate to falter and eventually to fail. Indeed signs of the fundamental difficulty appeared as early as that first private meeting between Briand and Stresemann at Thoiry just after they had proclaimed conciliation to a jubilant Assembly, blissfully unaware of what lay ahead for the League.

We shall never know precisely what occurred at the famous four-and-a-half-hour lunch at Thoiry, a small French village near Geneva. Stresemann's account differs in most particulars from that of Briand's interpreter, the only other person present.[12] Who offered what and who agreed to what are in dispute, but there is no doubt that both men were seeking a comprehensive settlement of all outstanding major issues between France and Germany. Stresemann apparently proposed complete evacuation of the Rhineland within a year, immediate return of the Saar, prompt withdrawal of the I.M.C.C., and repurchase of Eupen and Malmédy. In return he offered the possibility of commercialisation of part (or possibly eventually all) of the German reparations bonds under the Dawes

Plan so that France could receive immediate payment of a substantial amount of reparations.*

This extraordinary scheme has a certain aura of unreality. Normally Briand would not have listened to talk of immediate Rhineland evacuation and return of the Saar, while normally Stresemann would not have considered any action which would, for several technical reasons, render future reduction of the reparations debt more difficult. But Stresemann was taking advantage of a French financial crisis in hopes of purchasing Germany's freedom from the Versailles Treaty in return for a probably very limited debt commercialisation.

The opportunity arose from the fact that the French franc had collapsed, along with the Belgian franc and the Polish złoty, while the German mark was completely stabilised and American investments were flooding into Germany. In France years of heavy reconstruction costs, slipshod and deficit financing, and shrinking reparations had contributed to a débâcle so acute that in July 1926 Poincaré had been returned to power as Premier and Finance Minister, charged with the task of restoring the franc. Poincaré himself had authorised Briand to investigate commercialisation of reparations bonds as a route to some quick cash to save the situation. Stresemann seized the moment not only to treat with Briand but also to try to buy Eupen and Malmédy from Belgium and to announce that German participation in the financial reconstruction of Poland would be contingent upon immediate return of the Polish Corridor and Upper Silesia.[13] Of these the Franco-German plan alone did not involve outright territorial transfer from a victor power, but it did involve reparations, a matter of concern to other nations, notably Britain.

In the end the Thoiry scheme came to nothing as Poincaré briskly restored the franc through strict fiscal conservatism, while Belgian and Polish leaders did the same for their respective cur-

* Bonds payable over thirty-seven years representing mortgages on the German state railways and German industry were on deposit at the Reparations Commission. To commercialise these would be to effect a technical change in their status to that they could be marketed on the world's stock exchanges to private investors, chiefly American. Of the proceeds from any such sale, France would receive 52 per cent under the Spa Protocol of 1920. However, despite any future reductions of Germany's reparations liability, she would still owe the face value of the bonds to the private holders. For this reason and others, it seems improbable that Germany would have considered even gradual commercialisation of any appreciable amount.

rencies. In addition the Germans explored the drawbacks of commercialisation and the British objected strenuously to this prospect, if not to a revision of the Polish frontier. Besides all agreed that the American market could not absorb enough bonds to provide an appreciable cash yield. There was no real consensus on any of the terms of the Thoiry bargain and little prospect that both French and German opinion would accept any likely scheme. Within two months, as the franc began to recover its value, Briand abandoned the matter. Thereafter France and Germany returned to the more cautious approach of tackling their joint concerns one by one.

Ordinary citizens knew none of this, however. They were unaware that at Thoiry Briand and Stresemann were trying to do an improbable deal born of French financial desperation, or that they apparently agreed on none of the terms, or that Briand tackled Stresemann sharply about the numerous paramilitary organisations prevalent in Germany. The ordinary European knew only that, after the soaring oratory at Geneva, the French and German Foreign Ministers had smilingly wined and dined on rabbit stew together at a simple village inn and had sought to reconcile their national differences amicably. The spirit of Locarno appeared to have worked its magic.

This illusion was heightened for some by another event immediately thereafter. On 26 September 1926, barely a week after Thoiry, came announcement of the International Steel Agreement. This had been under negotiation since 1924 and undoubtedly would have reached fruition in any event, but it was viewed, except in some socialist quarters, as one more of the Locarno marvels. The agreement established a steel cartel* (called a steel pact to avoid wounding working-class sensibilities) involving Germany, France, Belgium, Luxemburg, and the Saar to limit production and thus raise prices. German industry particularly wanted such an arrangement, which provided penalties for exceeding agreed quotas and subsidies for underproduction. France on the other hand sought extension of duty-free entry of Lorraine iron ore into Germany (as allowed by the Versailles Treaty until 10 January 1925) in the face of threats of a high German tariff. The two agreements were negotiated concurrently and a Franco-German commercial treaty

* A cartel is a national or international arrangement among producers to control production, price, or distribution of a commodity.

was signed shortly after the steel cartel was established.[14] This, too, was hailed as yet another sign of the advent of true peace.

In the interim the steel cartel established its headquarters in the city of Luxemburg under the continuing chairmanship of the Luxemburgish members, thereby demonstrating the advantages of petiteness. Other cartels, chiefly to control metals, other minerals, chemicals, pharmaceuticals and munitions, were created in the ensuing months, while in 1927 Austria, Czechoslovakia and Hungary were admitted to the steel cartel *en bloc* with a single bloc quota. Britain and Poland declined to join on the terms offered. America, the world's largest steel producer, consumed her own production and so was no factor in European or world markets. Neither was Russia. But now most major continental producers had joined in an international agreement which, as the optimists noted, included three former Central Powers and their hitherto hostile neighbours.

The steel producers joined together primarily to increase their profits but some among them hoped that such arrangements could lay a foundation for a future European economic union. The cartel's first chairman, Emil Mayrisch, was an emphatic proponent of this view, and in its early years the steel cartel was thought by many to have profound implications for the future organisation of Europe. As the American economy boomed in the twenties, some of Europe's business leaders contemplated the advantages of mass production, mass markets, and large free-trade areas without restrictive tariffs, and talked of an economic 'United States of Europe'. They came to recognise that a small continent cut up into some thirty states, each with its own customs barriers, was not good for profits. And so the possibility of European union came to be contemplated seriously by hardheaded businessmen, not only by those whom they regarded as visionary cranks.

There also were the visionaries. Their headquarters was Vienna, their journal *Pan-Europa*, and their leader Count Richard Coudenhove-Kalergi, a Bohemian aristocrat of Czech citizenship and extraordinarily diverse ancestry. By October 1926 his movement had gathered sufficient momentum to hold a highly successful First Pan-European Congress in Vienna. The four days of meetings were jammed and the event was considered significant enough to evoke detailed reporting by professional diplomatists. The respectability which the movement had acquired, despite controversy over the specific views of its leader, who advocated reorganisation of the League on a regional basis, was indicated by the fact that the Austrian Chancellor opened the session, the considerably more powerful leader of the Austrian Catholic party made a speech of welcome, and Briand sent greetings, as did many prominent European politicians.

Not everybody was among the converted. Mussolini was so hostile that he sponsored a journal titled *Anti-Pan-Europa*. He was equally if less overtly hostile to both the League and Locarno. In January 1926, while Europe basked in the afterglow of Locarno, Mussolini declared that Fascism was embarking on its 'Napoleonic year.'[15] As usual Mussolini's oratory outran his performance, and the outcome in foreign policy hardly surpassed some of Napoleon III's less splendid years.

Mussolini's dislike of Locarno stemmed not only from the commitment involved but also from fear that pacification on the Rhine might turn German eyes to the Alps and Austria. Indeed Mussolini began his 'Napoleonic year' by an acrid public exchange in February with Stresemann over the rights of the German-speaking inhabitants of the South Tyrol (Alto Adige).* Mussolini favoured German nationalism provided that it remained on the Rhine and directed itself toward France, with whom Italy's relations were consistently strained as the two powers competed in North Africa and south central Europe. The Tyrolean tempest in a teapot, which lasted less than a month, enunciated Mussolini's concerns clearly. It also led to the resignation of the Secretary General of the Italian Foreign Ministry and, soon after, of several other key diplomatists. Thus such restraints as had existed dissolved and Mussolini was free to pursue his 'Napoleonic' designs.

The professional Italian diplomatists had in 1925 made a strenuous effort to arrive at a rapprochement with Yugoslavia over both Albania, a bone of contention beween them, and relations in general, primarily to forestall a Franco-Yugoslav treaty in the offing. Further they had urged Italian participation in a proposed 'Balkan Locarno' to ensure that it would not be directed against Italy. But Mussolini, who disliked the first Locarno, had no desire for a second. Instead, freed of diplomatic restraint, Mussolini pur-

---

* Mussolini's enthusiasm for Hitler derived in part from the fact that, alone among German nationalists, he was from the first prepared to abandon all claims on behalf of the south Tyrolese.

sued another course and in November 1926 signed the Treaty of Tirana with Albania.[16] This, the most solid diplomatic achievement of the Napoleonic year, did little more than formalise the existing Italian dominance in Albania. It was made possible by British acquiescence. Having just blocked any substantial Italian gains at the expense of Ethiopia and Turkey, Britain was glad enough to allow Mussolini a little balm for his ego in Albania which, from 1921 on, had been recognised by the Conference of Ambassadors as a special Italian sphere of interest.

As Mussolini had intended, the Treaty of Tirana put an end to all efforts toward Italo-Yugoslav rapprochement, and indeed thereafter he intrigued with Croatian separatists against Belgrade. The inevitable consequence was the completion of the Franco-Yugoslav treaty of friendship in November 1927.[17] As Romania had already signed a treaty of friendship with France in June 1926[18] and Czechoslovakia had a full-scale alliance dating from 1924, all members of the Little Entente were now tied to France. Briand held off the Yugoslav treaty for more than a year in hopes of coming to a tripartite French-Yugoslav-Italian arrangement and a general resolution of Italo-French tension arising from not only the Mediterranean and Danubian rivalry but also the vocal activities of anti-Fascist Italian *émigrés* in France. Ultimately, however, Briand recognised that Mussolini's hostility to Yugoslavia forced a choice between Italy and the Little Entente. He chose the Little Entente as the more reliable and less contentious partner.

Over the years the Little Entente had regarded Mussolini with a wary eye. Self-evidently he was interested in Danubia, domain of the Little Entente. In Mussolini's early years there had been some attempts at conciliation between Italy and the Little Entente countries, but relations with Czechoslovakia, a country much too democratic for Mussolini's taste, did not progress beyond a commercial treaty in 1924, while relations with Yugoslavia were strained first by Fiume and then by Albania. Moreover, accommodation with Romania was blocked by Mussolini's refusal to ratify the international accord recognising Romanian acquisition of Bessarabia, as he still hoped for major economic benefits from his early recognition of Russia. Beyond that the Little Entente was pained by Italy's generally good relations with Hungary and Bulgaria and by the latent revisionism in Mussolini's foreign policy.

From 1926 on that revisionism became more pronounced, and as the long-deferred Franco-Yugoslav treaty moved toward completion Mussolini made a futile attempt to counter French influence, disrupt the Little Entente, and reorganise Danubia under Italy's aegis. First he signed a treaty of friendship with Romania in September 1926,[19] close on the heels of the Franco-Romanian pact. The Italian treaty was singularly devoid of content but was designed as a step toward another. In 1927 Mussolini dangled before Romania the prospect of Bessarabian ratification in return for Italian economic penetration of Romania and a new quadruple alliance of Italy, Hungary, Romania and Bulgaria under Italian domination. Romania refused, having no desire to trade recognition of the Bessarabia *status quo* for the ominous threat of revision of the Transylvanian frontier implicit in any *rapprochement* with irredentist Hungary.

The net effect of Mussolini's effort to dismember the Little Entente was to draw it closer together and closer to France. It also repaired relations with Greece, despite continuing frontier incidents on the Greco-Yugoslav border, as on all Balkan frontiers. Mussolini was left with only the east-European revisionists, Bulgaria and Hungary. Bulgaria and Italy shared a common hostility to Yugoslavia, despite a pronounced restraint in Belgrade's reaction to Macedonian terrorist attacks on the Yugoslav-Bulgarian frontier. From 1926 on, Italy edged gradually closer to Bulgaria, offering her good offices to settle border incidents and to facilitate the international loan arranged in 1926 to resettle Bulgarian refugees from territories transferred to Greece by the peace treaties. While on a European tour in 1927 King Boris was treated to an audience with Il Duce.

Mussolini's actions towards Hungary were more dramatic. In April 1927 he signed a ten-year treaty of friendship, conciliation and arbitration, the first bilateral pact Hungary had gained with any of its wartime enemies.[20] This treaty, however, was the sum total of Hungary's diplomatic accomplishments in the era. Hungarian revisionism and hatred of the peace settlement rivalled the intense feeling in Germany, but Hungary had neither a Stresemann nor major-power status, and so Hungarian revisionism, even with Italian support, achieved little. For Italy the Hungarian treaty signalled the increasing revisionism of Italian policy, inherent in the Fascist stance from the first. In 1928 this revisionism was announced publicly, and Italy was charged at Geneva with smuggling munitions to Hungary in violation of the Treaty of Trianon.

None the less Mussolini's Napoleonic year or years had gained him little, perhaps in part as a consequence of Chamberlain's efforts to restrain him from major ventures and to appease him on minor issues. After thwarting Italian aims in Africa and the Near East in 1926 Chamberlain took care to entertain Mussolini on his yacht. Lady Chamberlain sported the Fascist insignia and the entire party offered the Fascist salute (except Chamberlain himself, prohibited by his position as a minister of the crown).[21] This did much for Mussolini's ego but nothing for his foreign policy. Lacking solid achievement Mussolini was left with little except an alignment with the weaker defeated nations of the war, a risky commitment to revisionism at the expense of France and the Little Entente, and an obligation in future to fulfil some of the expectations which his inflated oratory had aroused in Italy.

Mussolini's combination of great expectations and small accomplishments was not unique. In fact it could almost be taken as the pattern of events in the post-Locarno era. Whether on a multinational or a bilateral level, efforts toward genuine detente seemed doomed to almost perpetual disappointment. As peace had supposedly finally arrived, further disarmament appeared in order, and so two attempts were made to build upon the auspicious start of the Washington Naval Conference. On American initiative another naval conference was held in Geneva in June 1927, as the United States under President Calvin Coolidge hoped to extend the Washington limitations on capital ships to cruisers, destroyers and submarines. But tension between France and Italy was so acute that neither came, leaving only Britain and America to squabble at Geneva, with Japan futilely trying to play the peacemaker. The Anglo-American quarrel arose in part from British refusal to accept across-the-board American parity in all classes of ships, in part from widely different quota schemes arising from differing national interests and defence needs, and in part from lack of diplomatic preparation. Inexperienced American leaders, misled by the 1922 Washington success, failed to realise that, while it is possible to go the last mile at an international conference provided that much has been settled in advance and the will to agreement is strong, it is not possible to reconcile sweeping and fundamental differences in the glaring publicity of a short summit meeting. In the end the conferees had to take the unheard of step of disbanding without the slightest shred of accomplishment.[22]

In 1930 they tried again at London. Coolidge and the British Conservatives had gone; their replacements, Herbert Hoover and Ramsay MacDonald, prided themselves on their pacifism, humanitarianism and internationalism. The will to agreement was now stronger, and key issues had been settled in advance. In the autumn of 1929 MacDonald had invited himself to the United States, the first British Prime Minister to make the trip, and Hoover shrewdly took him off to his private fishing lodge on the Rapidan River in the mountains of Virginia. There, sitting on a log by the waterfalls, the two men ironed out Anglo-American naval differences, and MacDonald conceded parity in all classes to America.[23]

Despite the Rapidan agreement the London meetings the next year did not go much more smoothly than those at Geneva, although this time all five naval powers attended. Japan expressed dissatisfaction with the existing 10:10:6 ratio, especially in regard to cruisers. Italy insisted on parity with France over strenuous French objections, while France, in an effort to reinforce her sagging security, angled repeatedly for an American commitment. As Secretary of State Henry Stimson refused any commitment involving military aid and was equally cool to French proposals for an automatic trade boycott against aggressors, Britain also declined, for boycott leading to blockade and possibly to war against America could no longer be contemplated. Accordingly France and Italy refused to sign the naval agreement, which merely extended the building holiday on capital ships five years and established a 10:10:7 ratio across the board, except in submarines, where Japan gained parity, and in heavy cruisers, where Japan accepted the actuality of 10:10:7 under the paper appearance of 10:10:6. Further, Britain insisted upon an 'escalator clause' allowing a power to build beyond its quota if it felt threatened by a non-signatory (i.e. France or Italy), thus punching a large loophole in a limited agreement.[24]

Military disarmament fared even less well. From December 1925 on, a League of Nations Preparatory Commission laboured toward a world disarmament conference without making noticeable progress. Russia's call for an end to all armies, navies, and air forces met with resounding silence. France insisted upon security while Germany demanded equality, which France deemed incompatible with her security. Moreover Britain as a sea-power opposed large armies, the core of France's defence, and took issue with the French position on naval disarmament. A 1928 attempt to compose Anglo-French differences at the expense of the American view on naval vessels had to be abandoned in the face of intense Italian and American objections. Meanwhile, at Geneva the experts toiled slowly on toward the disarmament conference finally held in 1932, but even in the optimistic Locarno era, hard-headed diplomatists saw little prospect of accomplishment.

Attempts at international co-operation in the economic sphere met with similar scant success. By 1925 European agricultural and industrial production had returned to pre-war levels. Production continued to increase slowly throughout the remainder of the decade as stabilisation of currencies facilitated the exchange and thus the production of goods. But the increase in Europe's population combined with a sharp decrease in Europe's share of international trade and a slower economic growth rate than on other continents meant that Europe as a whole did not return to a pre-war standard of living. In general western Europe except Britain prospered and eastern Europe did not.

Even in the west there were serious economic problems and signs of stagnation. While the industrial nations of the west (including Germany and Czechoslovakia) maintained their technological superiority over the east, they faced severe competition from America. The western industrial powers invested heavily in eastern Europe and exploited the mineral resources of the Danubian region to their own profit, but western per capita income did not rise as it did in America. Investment capital for industrial modernisation was in short supply in the west, and these countries became heavily dependent upon infusions of American capital as their booming economies were increasingly fuelled by a stream of short-term American loans. Cartelisation continued apace, and the large European and American firms came to one arrangement after another, but still the European share of world markets continued to decline as Japan and America consolidated their wartime gains. In particular Britain's overseas markets shrank alarmingly. Beyond that European domestic markets were proving too small to absorb increasing production, but tariff barriers all over the continent inhibited exports.

In eastern Europe economic nationalism and high tariff barriers continued, along with growing agricultural distress. Overpopulation, small farms, and backward methods yielded inadequate and high-priced agricultural surpluses which could not compete with the endless bounty pouring into Rotterdam from the vast, modernised farms of America's heartland. While inexpensive river transport on the Danube meant that it was more economic for Austria to buy costly Hungarian or Romanian wheat than to trans-ship American grain from Rotterdam, the big population centres of western Europe found American wheat cheaper. Yet eastern Europe's only market for its agricultural produce was western Europe. As eastern Europe encountered difficulty in selling its crops in western markets, it was increasingly unable, despite French loans at high rates, to amass the foreign exchange it needed to purchase western Europe's industrial surplus.

Thus, even in the boom years, signs of economic stagnation were evident. Most efforts at international co-operation ran afoul of economic nationalism, but in May 1927 a three-week World Economic Conference was held at Geneva under League auspices. A thousand delegates and observers, mostly businessmen and economists, came from fifty nations all over the globe, including not only America but also Russia in her first formal appearance since Genoa. Russia's political and diplomatic isolation remained acute, but once again her economic potential ensured her presence at another economic conference. Despite the diverse representation at the conference, the emphasis was strongly European, although Russia and America shared the headlines. The Russian delegation protested vehemently against the heavy Swiss police guard imposed upon them to prevent their possible assassination by anti-communist Russian refugees, but, after much tense debate and a Russian threat to withdraw, gained official recognition of the existence of two economic systems, capitalist and communist, and of the possibility of their peaceful co-existence. The American delegates also found the atmosphere uncomfortable as European delegates envied the huge American internal free trade area, railed against high American tariffs, and talked variously of organising cartels against American economic might or of creating a United States of Europe to compete with Anglo-American domination of world trade. The conference had throughout a strong pan-European focus but could not agree on cartels or much else. In the end its final report was a damp squib, containing little more than exhortations to an all-out effort toward tariff reduction and a freer international exchange of goods.[25]

By the time a second Economic Conference met in Geneva in February 1930 optimism about what could be accomplished by efforts toward international co-operation had receded, and the agenda was confined to customs barriers as the chief impediment to trade. Still, the conference produced nothing more than a limited tariff truce, signed by the majority of European countries, freezing bilateral arrangements for one year. As a consequence of the conference, however, an agrarian bloc of eight east-European *cordon sanitaire* countries organised by Poland met in Warsaw in August 1930 to explore ways to combat agricultural depression and to improve the bargaining position of agricultural nations *vis-à-vis* the industrial giants. This group established a permanent organisation to concert agricultural policies and enjoyed a modest success until the dramatic economic and political changes of the 1930s rendered it a nullity.

The agrarian bloc was only one in a long series of Polish efforts in the Locarno years to improve her shaky international position and her almost uniformly unsatisfactory relations with her immediate neighbours. Poland's indifferent success well illustrates the limited options available to even a power of intermediate rank, particularly when the great powers interest themselves in its situation. Despite strenuous efforts by Skrzyński and, after Marshal Josef Pilsudski's *coup d'état* in May 1926, by his Foreign Minister August Zaleski, Polish relations with most of her neighbours remained strained while her international position became increasingly precarious.

One of the few Polish successes was with Czechoslovakia. As Skrzyński and Beneš both smarted from the sting of Locarno, they hastened to compose their differences. A treaty of arbitration and conciliation resulted, along with a commercial agreement. In addition a 1921 treaty with Romania was successfully renewed in March 1926.[26] As it reconfirmed Romanian possession of Bessarabia, however, it eliminated any faint hope of a Russo-Polish treaty, much to the relief of Stresemann, who had told Moscow that he would not sign the Treaty of Berlin if Russia came to terms with Poland. Skrzyński also made two efforts to reinforce Poland's position, first by a Scandinavian Locarno which Sweden and Finland refused, and then by a Baltic pact which Russia blocked to prevent Polish domination over the small Baltic states.

The advent of Pilsudski in 1926 brought political stability in the form of quasi-dictatorship, financial stabilisation, and relatively little reorientation of Polish foreign policy. He did relax the French tie to a degree, perhaps in recognition that its utility was declining rapidly as the Quai d'Orsay from 1927 on talked increasingly of revising the Polish frontier and became extraordinarily vague about the circumstances in which the Franco-Polish alliance would come into force.[27] Significantly the French had come to view this alliance more as a liability than as an asset. Significantly, too, the British quickly and the French more slowly came to recognise that the Polish frontier was untenable, for the simple reason that Germany would not accept it and Germany was a great power. Since no other great power was prepared to maintain that border by force, the Polish frontier was increasingly threatened. This trend continued as Germany's power position improved, Stresemann loudly championed German minorities in Poland at Geneva, Britain's small enthusiasm for the existing arrangement evaporated altogether, and Stresemann skilfully sapped French support. Thus Pilsudski and Zaleski struggled with little effect to find some accommodation between Germany and Russia and to come to terms with the other bordering states.

Of these Lithuania was utterly intransigent, and relations worsened into a dangerous crisis in 1927, after Augustinas Voldermaras seized power in Riga at the end of 1926. Germany and Russia, not wishing to see Polish influence extended, exhorted Lithuania to stand fast against efforts to resolve the crisis. Lithuania, who hardly needed urging, obligingly informed the League that she was threatened with invasion. Strenuous diplomatic efforts ended the technical state of war which had existed since the birth of both countries, but the border remained closed, and diplomatic relations were not established. Further efforts toward pacification failed, thanks to the natural hostility of the two parties and to the efforts of their two powerful neighbours who, as they said, continued to 'bet on the Lithuanian horse'.[28]

These two, Russia and Germany, constituted Poland's dilemma from the moment of her rebirth. The dilemma was deepened by the 1926 Treaty of Berlin which was in essence an anti-Polish pact based on the premise that Poland's frontiers should shrink at the first opportunity. While Russo-German economic and military ties continued to a degree throughout the late twenties, the two powers were no longer drawn together as outcasts since Germany had received full and Russia partial diplomatic rehabilitation. Their chief common concern now was eastern Europe in general, which Stresemann considered an exclusively Russo-German sphere of interest, and Poland in particular. As neither wished to see Poland settle with the other, in theory Polish diplomacy had a certain field of manoeuvre. In practice this field was sharply limited by the fact that Pilsudski could not seriously consider ceding the corridor and Upper Silesia to Germany and similarly could not contemplate any close embrace of the communist colossus equally eager to chew off territory.

None the less Pilsudski and Zaleski made a serious effort to improve relations with Russia. Some progress had been made when in May 1927 the Soviet envoy in Warsaw was assassinated by a Russian refugee. The ensuing war scare was sufficiently alarming to occasion a Locarno tea-party without Polish participation at Geneva in June. It also led to increased tension between Russia and Germany as Poland became a bone of contention between them. The difficulty was that, by this time, Russia needed the Russo-German tie far more than Germany did. Russia's diplomatic re-emergence remained limited. Relations with the western powers, always weak, had worsened. Indeed Britain, alarmed by Soviet propaganda and political meddling in England and throughout the Empire as well as Russian support of anti-imperialist movements in China, had just severed diplomatic relations altogether. Russia would not consider joining what she deemed to be a capitalist, imperialist League of Nations and she was not showered with invitations. In short, Germany was Russia's only entrée into the arena of great-power politics, a fact implicit in the Entente suggestion at the Locarno tea-party that Stresemann speak to Chicherin about Poland.

On the other hand Germany was a member in good standing of the League and the Locarno club, and thus had other options. While Stresemann appeared to give primary attention to Germany's western frontier, in fact he never took his eye off Poland, fully intending to regain Danzig, the Corridor, and Upper Silesia (and perhaps also Memel from Lithuania) at the earliest opportunity. He concluded, however, that revision of the Polish frontier could best be accomplished not through a deal with Russia but rather by simultaneously extracting France from the Rhineland, thus removing that brake on German freedom of action, and bringing Briand around to acceptance of frontier revision in the east. In the interim he made concessions to Pilsudski in small matters in order to allay his fears, and watched with equanimity a progressive decline in Russo-German collaboration.

As Stresemann bent himself to his task in the west, he, like Pilsudski and even more like Mussolini, found that the immediate post-Locarno years did not meet his expectations. Despite Mussolini's profound contempt for Stresemann, whom he erroneously considered insufficiently nationalistic, the two men had in common their intense revisionism and concomitant ambitious programmes which failed of rapid realisation. Stresemann's expectations were perhaps more justified and his skill certainly greater, but the fruits of Locarno did not ripen quickly enough to satisfy him. Unlike Mussolini he gained most of what he sought eventually, but it took longer than he had anticipated. One of several reasons for the delay was the fact that Austen Chamberlain's undoubted affection for Mussolini was equalled if not surpassed by his admiration for Briand and his frequent exasperation with Stresemann.

Stresemann had counted on British pressure to prod France to new concessions on the heels of German entry into the League. In both Berlin and London Britain's role was conceived of as an impartial arbiter between France and Germany and, in German eyes, impartiality meant speedy concessions. At the end of 1926 there did come promises to reduce the size of the occupation forces and to withdraw the I.M.C.C. altogether, as was done on 31 January 1927 without any close verification of German claims of fulfilment. There was also the *cachet* of the joint Nobel Peace Prize to the Locarno triumvirate, announced in December 1926. But that was all, and thereafter concessions came slowly, partly because there was no sustained British effort to hasten them. In part Britain's eyes were turned elsewhere, her chief concerns in the late twenties being strained relations with America, especially after the 1927 Geneva disarmament fiasco, the 1927 break with Russia, and the turbulent situation in China, where civil war and rising nationalism threatened British imperial interests to the point that she massed 20,000 troops at Shanghai in 1927 to defend the International Settlement there against Chinese assault. In part too, as Chamberlain admitted, he did 'love France like a woman'[29] and saw Briand as France's finest son. Thus he tended to veer between detente with

[handwritten margin note: Poincaré not mentioned]

Germany and entente with *la belle France*. Chamberlain developed a growing sympathy for Briand's domestic political problems, and thus reacted with increasing irritation against Stresemann's persistent and mounting demands for more concessions faster.

Like Stresemann, Briand had to contend with domestic opinion and, also like Stresemann, he made the most of it. France's craving for security had not abated, and the French generals in particular were adamant in insisting that the protective shield of the Rhineland occupation be retained as long as possible. As it must end eventually, the French military leadership, faced with a reduced term of military service and a falling birthrate, both portents of a smaller army in future, committed themselves in early 1927 to construction of the Maginot line, named for the then Minister of War. *[handwritten margin note: Maginot available]* This string of massive defensive fortifications along the German border from the Rhine to Belgium was not only reflective of French experience in the First World War but also designed ultimately to replace the protection afforded by the Rhineland occupation. The long debate in France over the costly Maginot project served chiefly to heighten the consciousness of insecurity of ordinary Frenchmen and thus to give the generals an opportunity for further pressure on Briand and the cabinet. Henceforth, until the Rhineland was actually evacuated in 1930, the military leaders never ceased to argue that it must be held until the Maginot Line was completed and France secure. They were joined by most of the right wing except Poincaré and by those who prophesied that evacuation would mean the end of reparations as well. Under these circumstances Briand, who was genuinely committed to pacification but not at the expense of France's safety, had little choice but to delay the dismantling of the barriers so carefully erected in 1919.

His foot-dragging began at once. Late in 1925 Stresemann had been promised troop reductions in the occupied territory and an early withdrawal of the I.M.C.C. Entente reluctance to take Germany's word without verification of fulfilment of the last remaining disarmament requirements, coupled with streams of intelligence reports, some of them exaggerated, about the excellence of the German army and paramilitary formations,[30] delayed the I.M.C.C. withdrawal until 1927. Troop reduction in the Rhineland proved an equally protracted matter, as French generals resisted and Briand thus could not agree with Chamberlain on the size of the reduction. In this matter Chamberlain leaned toward

Stresemann's view, but Briand, capitalising on Chamberlain's annoyance with Germany's 'ever-growing demands put forward almost as ultimatums',[31] succeeded in linking troop reduction to disarmament and thus in forestalling any reduction until September 1927. Even then, he held the cut to 10,000 men, leaving an occupying force of 60,000, predominantly French.

Stresemann did not consider these grudging and limited concessions adequate recompense for signing at Locarno and joining the League. At the Locarno tea-parties he never ceased to agitate for early evacuation of the Rhineland and return of the Saar. Periodically he would make use of his Russian weapon or mention the Polish border, preparing the ground ahead. On the immediate issues in the Rhineland, lack of progress led him to threaten resignation and to try to lure Chamberlain into unilateral evacuation. This effort to split the Entente failed, although it did rattle the teacups at Geneva, particularly in the spring of 1927.

Even Stresemann could not prevail against Anglo-French solidarity, and he had to wait. His patience was rewarded in 1928. The events of that year led to agreement at a Locarno tea-party during the League Assembly meetings in September that negotiations would begin over a final reparations settlement, an early evacuation of the Rhineland, and an agency of surveillance to ensure continuing demilitarisation of the area. While a promise to negotiate is a far cry from a completed agreement, it was a startling shift from haggling over the size of a troop cut to a sweeping reassessment of the only real restraints remaining on Germany: reparations and the Rhineland. Yet this shift was accomplished despite the illness of Chamberlain, which sent him off on a long cruise to the New World, and the more serious illness of Stresemann, which kept him away from Berlin and the direction of affairs for several months.

One impetus for the shift from small matters to large was a call in December 1927 from Parker Gilbert, Agent General for Reparations who supervised the workings of the Dawes Plan, for a new and final reparations settlement. As the Dawes Plan standard year, in which reparation payments would become onerous, would commence in September 1928, Germany soon took up the call. There was also growing concern that Germany was financing reparation payments from the abnormal flood of foreign investment into the country and could not continue to do so at a rising rate. Indeed there had developed a circular flow of money from private American investors into Germany, from Germany to the Entente powers, and from them to America in payment for war debts. As some specialists were increasingly aware, continuance of this monetary merry-go-round depended upon continuing American investment, which was beginning to slacken. Further, early in 1928 Stresemann ended his policy of restraint, declared German patience exhausted, and publicly demanded prompt evacuation of the Rhineland, calling the occupation an 'iron curtain' between France and Germany.[32] In response Briand hoped to trade early evacuation for a hard and fast reparations scheme and a Rhineland inspection system to enhance French security. Ultimately he failed. Inspection fell by the wayside, entombed in the Locarno arbitration clauses, and Stresemann successfully demanded evacuation as his price for accepting a vast reduction in Germany's reparation payments. Briand had been edged onto his path by Entente realisation that the spirit of Locarno was fading, that prolonged occupation meant increased bitterness, and that as the 1935 date for final evacuation came closer, the concessions obtainable in return for early withdrawal became fewer. Over the next year Stresemann made mincemeat of this logic, and the Entente made, not obtained, concessions in the course of the Rhineland negotiations.

One other factor perhaps facilitated the shift back to the concept of a comprehensive settlement. On 27 August 1928 the Kellogg–Briand Pact for the renunciation of war was signed in Paris. While much misunderstood by ordinary people at the time, the Pact refurbished the flagging spirit of Locarno, contributed to a renewal of the illusion that perpetual peace was at hand, and raised false hopes that America was emerging from isolation. Beyond that it gave Stresemann an opportunity to talk to Poincaré, who, in his concern for France's financial health, was eager for a reparations settlement even at the price of evacuation.

The Kellogg–Briand Pact, one of the great oddities of diplomatic history, arose originally from Briand's continuing concern for French security. He had forestalled major change temporarily, but could not do so indefinitely. Some sort of American commitment, however indirect, would reinforce France's weakening position. Accordingly in June 1927 Briand made the first of several overtures to this end and proposed that France and America bilaterally forswear war against each other. Secretary of State Frank Kellogg was unenthusiastic, viewing Briand's draft treaty as a negative guarantee forcing American neutrality should any of France's several allies embroil her in conflict. Pressures from American pacifist groups were strong, however, so in December Kellogg proposed instead a multilateral pact among the principal powers, excluding Russia. But, as France pointed out, most of these were bound by commitments to the League, Locarno, and guarantee treaties to make war in certain circumstances. Accordingly the draft text was diluted to allow for self-defence and fulfilment of treaty obligations and, at British request, the lesser Locarno powers, the Dominions, India, and Ireland were invited to participate. It was further understood that all other nations would be invited to adhere later.

After leisurely negotiation the final text of the International Treaty for the Renunciation of War as an Instrument of National Policy was ready for signature in the late summer of 1928.[33] It was a brief two-paragraph declaration against sin, devoid of any commitment or enforcement clauses. Thus Kellogg was willing to sign it. In addition to renouncing war as a national policy, the signatories agreed only that settlement of disputes would be 'sought' solely by peaceful means. One American senator sneeringly but accurately termed the treaty an 'international kiss'. Yet the Pact engendered immense enthusiasm among ordinary people without a sharp eye for enforcement clauses. While there are times when politicians gain votes by advocating war, the late twenties were not among them, especially in Europe. Peace was popular then, and the enthusiasm for the Kellogg–Briand Pact was indicative of a deep yearning to put the war and the postwar into the past and to enter upon a long, golden era of peace. Eager advocates convinced themselves that the flimsy foundation of the Pact was firm and that its empty verbiage could provide a genuine basis for true peace. In fact the Kellogg–Briand Pact contributed to the illusion of peace, not its reality, and proved completely ineffectual whenever it was invoked in the years to come. None the less, for all its defects, the Pact did constitute the first formal renunciation of war as an instrument of national policy in the annals of mankind and the first step toward the slowly spreading view that war is immoral.

One reason for the Pact's popularity was the mistaken notion that it signalled the return of America to world affairs. This illusion was heightened by the fact that Kellogg came to Paris to sign the treaty. Stresemann came too, arising from his sickbed with a nervous physician in attendance. As he was the first German Foreign Minister to visit Paris since the Franco-Prussian War of 1870, his presence added fuel to the flame of hope. On 27 August 1928, in an elaborate ceremony at the Quai d'Orsay dominated by the film technicians recording the event for posterity, distinguished representatives of fifteen nations signed the Pact with a special golden pen. Soon thereafter thirty-one more countries adhered. Almost everybody was delighted to declare against sin.

Russia was no exception. She not only signed but seized the moment to compensate for internal dissension and diplomatic weakness by an overture to Poland and an attempt to bolster Lithuania. Chicherin's deputy, Maxim Litvinov, proposed to both states that the Kellogg–Briand Pact be put in effect trilaterally among them without awaiting ratification by other powers. When Poland unexpectedly agreed, asking only for the addition of the other Baltic states and Romania, Stresemann took alarm, scenting a Russo-Polish rapprochement to the exclusion of Germany. However, the prompt ratification of the Pact by other powers robbed the Litvinov Protocol of 9 February 1929 of what little significance it possessed, and Russo-Polish relations soon deteriorated again, to Stresemann's considerable relief.

While in Paris for the signing ceremonies in August 1928, Stresemann saw Premier Poincaré, who later remarked on how seriously ill his old adversary was.[34] After Stresemann had assured Poincaré that he did not intend to raise the question of *Anschluss* as yet, despite much talk of it in Germany, they discussed Stresemann's most immediate concern, the Rhineland. He sought unconditional evacuation, but Poincaré indicated that evacuation must be contingent upon a reparations settlement.[35] Thus, despite some Anglo-French foot-dragging, the six nations of the Locarno tea-parties announced at Geneva on 16 September, in the absence of the ailing Stresemann and Chamberlain, that separate but parallel negotiations would begin on both issues plus the commission of verification proposed by Briand.

The Geneva communiqué of 16 September[36] called for a six-power commission of financial experts to devise a final reparations plan, as this task was considerably more complicated than early evacuation. This was to be the first but not the last 'final' plan, and henceforth there was much talk of 'final liquidation of the war'. As this in fact meant liquidation of the peace settlement and of the mentality which created it, Germany took the lead in calling for the committee of experts and urged inclusion of American citizens, partly because war debts to America were bound to be a consideration and partly because Americans, with few direct claims on Germany, might be moderate. While the American government was unenthusiastic about even private American participation, it agreed that Owen D. Young, a banker whose involvement with reparations dated back to the Dawes Plan, would chair the committee, many of whose other members were equally experienced in the arcane mysteries of reparations.

The Young Committee began work early in 1929 and concluded its labours in June. By then the Locarno triumvirate had met together during League Council sessions at Lugano to try to resolve the political issues. Chamberlain had backed Briand's insistence on a verification mechanism, his view that the second or Coblenz Rhineland zone (scheduled for evacuation in January 1930) be evacuated only when negotiations on security and reparations had made real progress, and his demand that withdrawal from the third (Mainz) zone be contingent upon a final reparations settlement. Thereafter Briand's position stiffened and he refused to discuss evacuation at all until the Young Report was received. Instead he came increasingly to Poincaré's opinion that evacuation should be gradual as reparations under the new plan were commercialised and advance payment received by France. This stand became more difficult to maintain through the months as the experts laboured to draft the plan because, across the Channel, Chamberlain found his foreign policy under mounting attack. The Labour and Liberal parties called loudly for immediate, unilateral, unconditional evacuation of the Rhineland. Chamberlain held firm but, in the May 1929 general election, the Conservatives lost their majority. On 5 June a new Labour government took office under MacDonald, with Arthur Henderson as Foreign Secretary.

The new government, which quickly restored relations with Russia, found itself immediately faced with the Young Report of 7 June 1929.[37] This document had been achieved with great difficulty as there was no agreement between what the creditors hoped to receive and what Germany deemed to be her capacity to pay. The plan enshrined Entente expectations on paper but not in practice. It specified that Germany pay annuities in varying amounts, all below the Dawes standard-year figure of 2500 milliard marks, for 59 years, the duration of Allied debt payments to America. The paper total, covering all charges including service of the Dawes loan, came to nearly 114 milliard marks, but had a present marketable value of only about 37 milliard marks. If paid in full the annuities would cover war debts and provide most countries except Britain with some indemnity. However, only 660 million marks of each annuity (generally about one-third) was unconditionally payable, and only this portion of the debt could be commercialised. The remainder was postponable under certain conditions of economic or monetary distress. Thus the gap between expectations and potential economic reality was papered over.

While Germany was not pleased with the ostensible total, she had succeeded in keeping the annuities for the first ten years all below two milliard marks. Before that time lapsed, surely there would be an end to reparations or at least another reduction. In the interim deliveries in kind would be sharply reduced and all supervision of German finances would end. Further, the complex structure of treaty commissions and Dawes Plan agencies would be dissolved. In their place a Bank for International Settlements would be established at Basle, Switzerland, charged to receive and distribute reparation payments and to provide a long-needed institution for co-operation among central banks of various countries.* In its second function the Bank still survives, an essential pillar of the European Economic Community and the sole legacy of reparations.

Germany accepted the Young Plan because the only alternative was continuance of the much higher Dawes payments, but at the same time demanded full and immediate evacuation of the Rhineland and return of the Saar as the price of acceptance. France also accepted the Plan but not evacuation before payment was received, nor any discussion of the Saar. Britain on the other hand, while backing France on the Saar, threatened unilateral evacuation and refused to approve the Young Plan without modification. Instead of attempting to compose these yawning differences, the three powers convened in early August, along with Italy, Japan and Belgium, at The Hague for what they grandly titled 'The Conference on the Final Liquidation of the War'.

---

* For example, the Bank of England, Bank of France, Bank of Italy, and so on. In America's decentralised system, the Federal Reserve Bank of New York fulfils the functions of a central bank in international monetary matters.

The month-long first Hague Conference, as it is more commonly called, was almost entirely consumed by the successful British effort to modify the Young Plan to British advantage. The extraordinarily acerbic Chancellor of the Exchequer, Philip Snowden, conceded neither a farthing nor a polite word, loudly protesting the revision of the old Spa percentages in the Young Plan, which left Britain with her war debts covered but no reparation for damage done. While this bore some resemblance to the Balfour note of 1922, Snowden was adamant, particularly since Britain's share of the unconditional annuities was to be slight. Agreement on political questions was equally difficult as Briand insisted on verification of demilitarisation and Stresemann demanded the Saar, while Henderson declared that, whatever else happened, British troops would be home by Christmas, but Briand maintained that the French army must stay another year. On every political issue it was two against one and the majority won. Briand had to settle for ephemeral verification while Stresemann had to accept later talks on the Saar, which came to nothing. While not conceding fully to Anglo-German pressure, Briand also had finally to agree that the Rhineland would be free of foreign troops by 30 June 1930. On the financial question, however, majority rule failed in the face of Snowden's flinty stance. After weeks of wrangling, the Young reparations receipts were reallocated to British benefit.

When the major disputes were settled, no time remained to draft enabling documents and resolve lesser details, as the diplomatic timetable required that the Foreign Ministers arrive at Geneva within forty-eight hours for the annual Assembly meeting. Accordingly the conferees hastily organised themselves on their final day, drafted a Protocol of 31 August 1929 accepting in principle the decisions reached, and belatedly chose a chairman, Prime Minister Henri Jaspar of Belgium, who was charged with appointing committees to complete the work of the conference and reconvening it when all was arranged.[38]

Six days later at Geneva Briand issued a dramatic call for European union, urging not only economic association but also a degree of political and social federation. As the old sanctions were dissolving, Briand attempted to enmesh Germany in a new web of European integration, creating an interdependence which might in time eliminate war as a practical possibility. While German and British press reaction was cool, Stresemann himself was gracious.

In what proved to be his last diplomatic appearance, he ruled out the unspoken thought of some that a European bloc could serve as an instrument of economic war against America, but gave his blessing to steps to bring Europe out of economic obsolescence. It was agreed that Briand would draft a proposal, that the twenty-seven European members of the League would consider and amend it, and that a revised draft would be further discussed at Geneva in a year's time.

Meanwhile the British and Belgians had already begun their withdrawal from the Coblenz zone in the Rhineland and the French their retirement into the Mainz zone. Both were completed before Christmas. By then hostility to the Young Plan in Germany had reached disturbing proportions, expressing itself in a national plebiscite in which 5·8 million voters registered opposition.[39] While this raised some questions about future German good faith, the sole guarantee of fulfilment embodied in the Plan, it was insufficient to overturn German ratification. Accordingly the seven committees convened by Jaspar, one of them revealingly termed the 'Committee on Liquidation of the Past', completed their tasks and he issued a call for a second conference at The Hague on 3 January 1930.

In the interim Stresemann had died on 3 October 1929, having literally worked himself to death at the age of fifty-one. In his last months he had recognised the rising tide of strident, belligerent German nationalism and had known that the days of his indirect and patient policy were numbered. Had he lived he undoubtedly would have tried to stem this clamorous tide long enough to regain the Saar, a task to which no other German leader was equal. None the less, in his six years as architect of German foreign policy, he had liberated the Ruhr and the Rhineland, ended military inspection, twice reduced reparations, and transformed Germany from the pariah to the pre-eminent member of the European family of nations. He had further demonstrated the futility of imposing upon a great power a treaty which it will not accept. Germany's absolute refusal to accept had always been the chief difficulty with the Versailles Treaty. Stresemann had broken most of the fetters. His successor, Julius Curtius, bent himself with lesser skill to completing the task.

Fortunately for the inexperienced Curtius, Germany was not the main issue at the second lengthy Hague Conference. As the Young

Committee had called for the dissolution of the joint reparations responsibility of the wartime Central Powers, the conference sought a comprehensive settlement of non-German reparations. Since the seven successor states to the old Habsburg Empire had inherited its debts and five of them were entitled to reparations from the other two, the potential for discord was immense and fully exploited. But smaller states, unlike Germany, could be threatened into compliance. After less than three weeks of major power pressure, a huge heap of documents were solemnly signed on 20 January 1930. These formally closed the old pre-Dawes accounts, thus cancelling the reparations clauses of the Versailles Treaty, regulated non-German reparations, provided for the evacuation of the Rhineland, and, along with a variety of special bilateral agreements and annexes, arranged the entrance into force of the modified Young Plan.[40] As the experts had planned for it to go into effect on 1 September 1929, it was made retroactive to that date. In fact by common consent the Young figures had been quietly applied immediately after the first Hague Conference and Germany was currently paying less than half of what she would have owed under the Dawes Plan. For this reduction, her reward was the Rhineland.

The last French troops left German soil precisely as scheduled on 30 June 1930. The next day President Hindenburg, together with the entire German Cabinet, issued a proclamation in honour of the occasion.[41] In deference to the growing forces of right-wing nationalism it conspicuously omitted mention of Stresemann, undoubted father of the liberation. Instead, in a document full of nationalist fervour, the proclamation spoke pointedly of Germany's obligation to her war dead, and called for the return of the Saar. At once the paramilitary veteran's organisation, the *Stahlhelm*, with which Hindenburg publicly associated himself, engaged in jubilant demonstrations on the French and Belgian borders in the demilitarised zone.[42]

Despite these disturbing portents, which led the British ambassador, Sir Horace Rumbold, to write of German 'ingratitude and tactlessness',[43] Briand's plan for European union was under active consideration through the summer. In May he had circulated a detailed proposal calling for a federation based on moral union and regional entente reinforced by permanent legislative, executive, and secretarial institutions.[44] Briand noted that he was placing political matters before economic as economic union depended upon security which in turn was linked to political union. In brief he was attempting to reinforce the existing political *status quo*. Not surprisingly Briand called for a general European system of arbitration, security and Locarno-style international guarantees. He briefly urged the creation of a European common market with free circulation of capital, goods and peoples, but suggested that detailed economic proposals, along with the possibilities of intellectual and parliamentary co-operation, be deferred for later study.

This proposal, so clearly designed to substitute a new peace structure for the old, was under active debate by the European members of the League gathered at Geneva for the annual Assembly meeting when on 14 September 1930 Adolf Hitler's Nazi Party scored its smashing victory in the German Reichstag election, coming from nowhere to gain 107 seats and become the second largest party. With rare realism, the League Assembly referred Briand's plan to a committee for quiet interment. While the illusion of permanent peace was not yet shattered, it had developed a conspicuous crack and henceforth those charged with guarding the security of European states watched with deepening dismay as this crack spread across the entire fragile façade, portending disintegration to come.

5 The Crumbling of Illusion

DECADES rarely provide convenient historical dividing lines, but 1930 was something of a watershed year. It would be an oversimplification to suggest that the twenties looked back to the First World War while the thirties looked ahead to the Second World War. None the less the diplomacy of the twenties had centred on the postwar settlement and attempts to uphold or undo it, with a mounting desire to consign the postwar bitterness to history. The Hague Conference's Committee on the Liquidation of the Past was only one of many signs of a widespread belief that old problems could be solved with a consequent reinforcement of peace and prosperity. As the decade turned with many of the old problems unresolved, Europe entered into an era of new problems, economic and political, including immediate fears of a new war. In response to the German election returns of 1930 a French politician remarked, 'We've been outwitted'[1] and the Belgian Foreign Minister nervously expressed 'great fears of an imminent fresh outbreak of war'.[2]

Unfortunately there had been widespread hope that 'liquidation of the past' meant the end of all problems. Henceforth peace, prosperity and international harmony would reign. Indeed the late twenties had been a period of surface harmony and apparent economic prosperity Except in Britain, whose economic ailments seemed incurable, the western industrial world had enjoyed a considerable economic expansion and, in some areas, a rising standard of living. These trends had been particularly pronounced in Germany and America, fuelled in both instances by American investment. Why should not these good times continue? The Young Plan was in fact predicated upon the premise that German and western expansion would continue indefinitely. Similarly it was widely believed that, with the Rhineland evacuation and a 'final' all-European reparations settlement, there would be little future occasion for international tension, at least in Europe. After all,

Russia had adhered to the Kellogg–Briand Pact, Mussolini had not engaged in any escapades for several years, the Balkans and the Baltic were less turbulent than usual, and the greatest single source of Franco-German tension had been removed. Surely after so many years of strain and tension, one could expect that true peace had come.

Yet warning signs had been flashing for several years for the shrewd to see. In many Foreign Ministries it was recognised that the postwar settlement had been based on a particular power balance and that the more the balance shifted the more the settlement would be revised. Hence growing Polish nervousness. Moreover the clamorous voices of revisionism and of intense nationalism were steadily rising higher, both in Europe and in Asia. In general the dissatisfied powers were becoming stronger and more aggressive, leading the thoughtful to wonder what lay ahead.

One of the few dissatisfied powers which was not becoming stronger was China, and her weakness of itself created a dangerous situation. While the Chinese nationalist, anti-imperialist, and anti-foreign movements continued unabated, so did the multi-faceted Chinese civil wars. As these became increasingly complex, particularly after the most effective nationalist general, Chiang Kai-shek, broke with the Communists in 1927 and expelled the numerous Russian advisers, a dangerous power vacuum developed, especially on the outer fringes of the roiling Chinese mass where none of the competing Chinese governments could for long maintain much effective control. Inevitably such a situation put temptation before powerful and aggressive neighbours.

Among those tempted was Japan, whose revisionism was becoming increasingly pronounced. In an era when further disarmament was the watchword Japan displayed acute displeasure with the outcome of the 1930 London Naval Conference, whose results, so favourable to Japan, did not satisfy her. Japan clearly needed mainland markets and raw materials in areas nominally controlled by China, and her economy, so dependent upon international trade, would obviously be highly sensitive to world market fluctuations. Further, tension was growing steadily between the military authorities and the civilian governments. Should the military win the *sub rosa* struggle in progress, there was little doubt that Japan's policy would become aggressive.

Russia kept a wary eye on both these Asian neighbours but, after her expulsion from China, an even warier eye on Europe. Stalin devoted the late twenties to tightening his control of Russia and to headlong industrialisation. As his grip on power became more secure, some wondered how long he would rest content with the boundaries forced on a prostrate Russia at war's end. Stalin himself watched Germany and was among the first to react to the warning signs there. Even before the German election he recognised that Russo-German collaboration was moribund and signalled a policy switch in July 1930 with the appointment of Litvinov as Foreign Commissar to replace the ailing Chicherin. Litvinov pursued a policy of co-operation with the west-European powers and with Geneva. While Russia did not as yet join the League, Litvinov regularly attended special conferences held under its auspices at Geneva and cultivated the confidence of western leaders. As Hitler's electoral successes swelled and his anti-semitic oratory evoked wide response in Germany, Litvinov, who was Jewish, remained in office and, from 1932 on, Stalin took care to ensure that Russia's new factories were situated in or east of the Ural mountains, beyond the range of German bombers. In 1932 as well, Russia signed non-aggression pacts with France and with four of her north-European neighbours, including Poland. Having mended his diplomatic fences, Stalin consolidated his power in Russia and watched.

Mussolini also watched and consolidated his position, both at home and in Albania. In the late twenties he eliminated most political opposition in Italy and reinforced his dictatorship. He also enjoyed his greatest diplomatic achievement, which proved to be his sole important legacy. By the Lateran Accords of 11 February 1929,[3] he ended the cold war between the Italian kingdom and the papacy dating from the unification of Italy in 1870. These three treaties established the sovereign state of the Vatican City in Rome (area 108·7 acres), provided financial compensation to it for the seizure of the Papal States by Italy in 1870, and defined the special status of the Roman Catholic religion in Italy. While Mussolini's success in ending an absurd situation arose largely from being in power at the right moment, the Lateran Accords brought him new popularity and facilitated a firmer grip upon Italy. In the international arena Mussolini's respectability quotient, already high, soared higher, and much twaddle was written about a spiritual renaissance in Italian fascism.

Otherwise, after his failure to disrupt the Little Entente, Mussolini's foreign policy was largely confined to distinctly unspiritual sabre-rattling and to an attempt at economic penetration of Ethiopia. Relations with France remained consistently poor, and Mussolini scarcely bothered to conceal his contempt for Briand's attempts toward international conciliation and European union. Despite Britain's best efforts, France and Italy could not be brought to any agreement on naval limitations as Mussolini was adamant in his insistence on parity. Since France had a much larger fleet in being, along with north and south Atlantic coastlines and Asian colonies to defend, all of which Italy lacked, Mussolini's determination to enlarge his navy heralded aggressive plans for the future. By 1930 this quarrel and Mussolini's increasingly bellicose oratory had generated a widespread belief that Italy had become the leader of the revisionist states.[4] Still Il Duce did little. Like Stalin he watched, alert to any threat to Austria from Germany and to the possibility that this vital buffer might be erased by Anschluss.

The mere fact that Anschluss was being actively talked about and worried about in 1930 was only one of many signs of mounting German revisionism. Throughout the year the German appetite grew, unslaked by the Rhineland evacuation. Hindenburg's proclamation on that occasion was an indication of increasing revisionism, as was the intense protest against the Young Plan. In addition the weakness of the Weimar political system was becoming glaringly obvious as, from July 1930 on, the Reichstag rarely met because the Cabinet of Chancellor Heinrich Brüning could rarely command a majority and increasingly resorted to rule by presidential emergency decree. Then too, German military and naval expenditures had been rising sharply and continued to rise, although Germany claimed that her army and navy remained within the stringent limits laid down by the Versailles Treaty. Western military attachés consistently doubted these claims and noted that the German army, whatever its exact size, was being trained as the cadre for a much larger army.[5] Foreign observers were less likely to notice the quiet growth and organisational development of the Nazi party in the late twenties, as it spread from Munich throughout Germany and acquired a solid base for future expansion.

The economic scene also provided warning signs, particularly in Germany, and a few of these were heeded. The Young Plan, with its sharp cutback in annual payments, was in part precipitated by realisation that American investment was slowing as more lucrative opportunities developed in the United States. While in the late twenties Germany did borrow in order to pay reparations and repay debts, she also borrowed in order to live lavishly. Germany borrowed nearly twice as much as she paid in reparations and much of the balance, often borrowed by municipalities, was expended on football (soccer) stadia, swimming pools complete with artificial wave-making apparatus, [6] and blocks of workers' housing containing the unheard-of extravagance of private bathrooms in each family unit. While there was some sarcastic grumbling from Britain and France, for such luxuries were rare among the working classes of the European victors, there was also an envious desire to emulate the German boom. But this boom, despite Germany's fundamental economic strength, rested on a fragile base consisting of borrowing and more borrowing, largely in the form of short-term loans which could be recalled on ninety-days notice or on demand. The debts mounted, but the danger of using short-term loans for long-term building projects was blithely ignored. By 1928 American investment slackened and, after the New York stock market crash in 1929, slackened more. Then came the 1930 German election.

As the American crash, heralding the advent of a world-wide depression of unprecedented severity, occurred in the autumn of 1929 and the German election with the smashing Nazi victory occurred in the autumn of 1930, it has been commonplace to assume that the depression was responsible for Hitler's triumphant march to power. This assumption is no doubt comforting, implying as it does that only in extraordinary circumstances of overwhelming calamity could a civilised European nation embrace such unparalleled barbarism. Alas, it is inexact. Despite the sudden drama of the New York crash, the depression was a slowly creeping miasma, which arrived gradually over several years. Even in America where it all began rock bottom was not reached until March 1933, two months after Hitler became Germany's Chancellor.

During the summer of 1930, as the electoral campaign was in progress, the German economy was in a recession but not yet a depression. Nobody was suffering much except the workers, who remained true to their traditional parties. [7] Fear of a depression undoubtedly moved some members of the middle class, so badly traumatised by the 1923 inflation, to vote Nazi, especially since the economic misery of 1923 was generally blamed on France and the Versailles Treaty, and the Nazis loudly proclaimed that they alone had never endorsed anything done under the Versailles *diktat*. Even so, one must conclude that, while the Weimar Republic had its economic ailments in 1930, its mortal illness was virulent nationalism.*

Foreign policy dominated the electoral campaign. In a justly celebrated dispatch, Rumbold, a shrewd and moderate observer, surveyed the German political scene and remarked that calls for repeal of the Young Plan, ratified only in March, came from clear across the political spectrum. In part this rare unanimity reflected popular belief that the reduced Young annuities were responsible for the recession, and in part it reflected the view, widely evident even in 1929, that any further reparations were an insult to German honour. Rumbold also noted demands from left, right, and centre for immediate return of the Saar, immediate revision of the eastern frontier at Polish expense, return of the pre-war colonies, and rearmament. He concluded:

The snowball of 'revisionism' continues to roll down the electoral slopes, and, as it rolls, it is gathering speed and size. It may now indeed be said that the first electoral campaign which has taken place in Germany without the shadow of the Rhineland occupation has brought out into the open, through one party or another, all that Germany hopes for and intends to strive for in the field of external affairs. [8]

Rumbold unerringly put his finger on the key factor: the Rhineland evacuation. The occupation, with French troops across the Rhine in the Coblenz and Mainz bridgeheads, had been a club held over Germany's head, necessitating the patient indirect policy of Stresemann. With the removal of this club, twelve years of pent-up nationalist fervour exploded, sending $6\frac{1}{2}$ million voters to the support of Adolf Hitler in the hope of eliminating the last remaining vestiges of the 1918 humiliation and restoring the glories of pre-war Germany, colonies and all.

As it is simplistic to argue that the depression caused Hitler's

* In this connection, it should be noted that in November 1932, when the depression had become genuinely acute in Germany and the onset of winter was making a severe situation worse, the Nazi vote dropped significantly.

accession to power, so it is even more simplistic to argue that Hitler's 1930 victory caused the depression. None the less, the sudden Nazi surge did accelerate the advent of the depression in central Europe and heighten its severity there. After the election the Brüning government tried to counter the Nazi threat by embarking on a more aggressive foreign policy, particularly in regard to Austria. This set off within eight months a chain reaction of banking crises from Austria to Germany and eventually to Britain. More immediately the reaction of investors to the German election was swift. The Berlin stock exchange plummeted downward and there ensued a massive withdrawal of capital from Germany as the short-term notes were called in. Within three months at least 1·3 milliard marks were withdrawn, over a third of the foreign exchange then invested in Germany and the equivalent of about three-quarters of the 1930–31 Young annuity. French, Belgian, Swiss, and American financiers withdrew their loans while German liberals and German Jews sent their funds to safety elsewhere. Few new credits appeared to replace the old. While the German economic crisis was of manageable proportions in August 1930, by December the situation had become acute as unemployment soared. And in the winter of discontent, depression and misery, the year turned, ushering in what Arnold Toynbee soon was to term '*annus terribilis*'.[9] ✳

1931 was aptly named. It proceeded from calamity to calamity, all of them terrible. The year began with a crisis over the prospect of *Anschluss*, shaking the foundations of both the Paris peace settlement and the fragile financial structure of central Europe. The spreading stain of the depression crept onward, with occasional sudden lurches into the abyss of major banking failures and concomitant business bankruptcies, causing more unemployment. The black cloud of the Nazi menace loomed ever larger and more thunderous. Meanwhile in an extraordinary irony of mistiming, plans for the long-heralded 1932 disarmament conference also crept along, the planners themselves trying to overlook mounting German, Italian and Japanese militancy, along with obvious Russian and German rearmament. Neither to the diplomatists nor to the politicians did it occur that rearmament was the swiftest cure for unemployment and depression. On the contrary in most countries, as tax revenues fell, government expenditure was cut, thus increasing unemployment and reducing tax revenues further. Finally, *annus terribilis* closed with a bang, a shooting war in the Far East, demonstrating to those who still cherished hopes that the League of Nations could not keep the peace. All in all *annus terribilis* destroyed many illusions. When it ended, while few could envisage the full horrors ahead, there was no longer any talk of an extended era of peace and prosperity. Instead increasing numbers of people were asking whether western civilisation could endure.

When *annus terribilis* began the European world was still optimistically discussing disarmament. As government budgets shrank it seemed only reasonable that armaments should be the first category of expenditure to be slashed. Thus hopes remained high at Geneva although, in the Foreign Ministries, hardheaded diplomatists were doubtful, noting the continuing Franco-Italian naval squabble and the fact that Germany was building an extraordinary new warship with plans for more to follow. The *Deutschland*, launched with full ceremonial by Hindenburg on 19 May, was a pocket battleship (or heavy cruiser) and a triumph of naval engineering. While technically within the Versailles Treaty limitations, it combined such speed and firepower that it could sink any ship afloat speedy enough to catch it and outrun any ship powerful enough to sink it. Funds for a sister ship (Cruiser B) were voted by the Reichstag on 20 March 1931 and plans for a third (Cruiser C) were well advanced. Throughout the tangled crises of reparations, loans, Austrian alarms, and rearmament which dominated the remainder of the year, the Brüning government steadfastly refused to delay construction of Cruiser B or jettison plans for Cruiser C, explaining when necessary that the project was particularly dear to the heart of the 'Old Gentleman'.[10]

The voting of funds for Cruiser B stirred the chanceries of Europe only moderately because the first major crisis of *annus terribilis* erupted the next day and immediately engulfed lesser matters. 21 March brought official confirmation of mounting rumours about a project for an Austro-German customs union. This proposal had been under desultory consideration since February 1930 but had been given new impetus by Austria's economic plight and Germany's political condition. Throughout Austrian motives were economic, including overtures to France and Italy, while German motives were political. Not only was Brüning eager to steal Nazi thunder and Curtius to set Germany astride the Danube, but also there was a wider aim to dominate central Europe, strangle Poland economically, and then force political concessions from her, liberating what State Secretary Bernhard von Bülow of the German Foreign Ministry called 'occupied territories'.[11]

The treaties of Versailles and Saint-Germain both forbade *Anschluss*. While a customs union was not *Anschluss*, it was universally regarded as a giant step in that direction. Moreover the 1922 Geneva Protocol for Austria's financial reconstruction had explicitly forbidden any measure affecting Austria's economic independence. Accordingly the Vienna Protocol of 19 March 1931 embodying the customs union project was drafted with a careful eye to circumventing these restrictions. In addition the Vienna Protocol was a fully completed treaty slightly rephrased to look like a mere draft proposal in hopes of soothing the susceptibilities of foreign leaders to whom no warning had been given that such a bombshell would burst. Finally, the announcement was timed to coincide with the meeting of the committee considering Briand's plan for European union in order to give the customs union project an aura of respectability. As von Bülow had said, 'We will dress the matter up with a pan-European cloak.'[12]

Nobody was deceived, and the startling absence of diplomatic preparation drew a sharp reaction. France in particular took alarm and was in a position to take action, especially since her currency was now the strongest on the continent. Protests to Germany were unavailing as Brüning threatened his own resignation and the advent of Hitler in an effort to carry the customs union, so pressure was put on the weaker partner. In early April an Austrian request for a French loan immediately gave rise to political conditions, including an Austrian promise to postpone further negotiations on the customs union. As efforts toward a common front with Britain failed, France combined the carrot and the stick, offering loans, concessions and cartels in return for an end to Austro-German revisionism. Germany turned a deaf ear, but Austria was in no position to do so. On 11 May the Creditanstalt, largest of Austrian banks, in whose direction French interests were conspicuous, reached a state of virtual collapse. While French action had not caused its difficulties, which stemmed from earlier failures of smaller banks before announcement of the customs union, France may have affected the timing of disclosure of the failure. As the Creditanstalt's balances constituted three-eighths of the total holdings of all Austrian banks combined and 70 per cent of all Austrian commerce and industry depended heavily upon it, it could not be permitted to close its doors, but massive Austrian government intervention to save it inevitably led to an appeal under the 1922 Geneva Protocol for additional loans to stave off another national bankruptcy. Thus in short order, the Austrian financial crisis linked the customs union project to its chief obstacle, the 1922 Protocol.

Not surprisingly Austria soon lost heart, especially as France, the primary source of new loans, insisted in a three-hour ultimatum upon abandonment of the customs union. Germany remained truculent despite her own mounting financial crisis. In the end, despite German objections, the legal questions surrounding the customs union were referred to the Permanent Court of International Justice at The Hague. On 5 September, in a decision based more on legal than on political considerations, the Court narrowly ruled by a vote of eight to seven that the Vienna Protocol did not violate the Treaty of Saint-Germain but, by the same vote, that it did violate the 1922 Geneva Protocol.[13]

By then the customs union project was thoroughly dead, but, in the interim, its repercussions had heightened the European financial crisis as the Creditanstalt collapse triggered a further dramatic flight of capital from both Germany and Austria. The Bank of England rushed to Austria's rescue with short-term loans which only exacerbated Britain's own financial crisis late in the summer, causing the credits to be withdrawn in August. Germany's close association with Austria generated a new rush to withdraw credits, culminating in a German banking crisis in July. As the flight of both German and foreign capital intensified, the German government began a vehement informal agitation for reparations relief while throughout refusing any concessions on the customs union, Cruiser B, or the army budget, which was nearly triple that of Britain. German leaders believed that the alarm of private American investors over the German credit crisis could be exploited to reduce reparations. Tending to blame all distress on reparations rather than on German financial and political practices or worldwide economic trends, the German Cabinet campaigned through May and June for revision of the Young Plan, to the further detriment of German credit. An extraordinarily pessimistic government manifesto on 6 June only accelerated the credit débâcle.

American investors were indeed alarmed, not only the huge New York banks which had committed so much capital in Germany but middle western and New England financial consortia which also had invested heavily. As the German credit crisis had reached proportions endangering the American banking structure, and as a psychological victory over the depression was sorely needed, on 20 June Hoover unilaterally proposed a one-year moratorium commencing on 1 July for all intergovernmental debts, stating that: 'The American Government proposes the postponement during one year of all payments on intergovernmental debts, reparations and relief debts, both principal and interest, of course not including obligations of governments held by private parties.'[14]

While cancellation of war debts remained politically impossible, postponement was feasible, particularly to ensure the safety of private investment. In a sense, for all creditor nations, namely America and those Allies receiving German reparations, private investments were put ahead of public accounts and the immediate interests of the ordinary taxpayer. While self-interest in Wall Street and the City of London contributed considerably to this decision, it must equally be remembered that a massive Anglo-American banking collapse would have brought untold misery throughout the world.

There were several difficulties with Hoover's proposal. Its sudden announcement without diplomatic preparation, while arising from domestic American political considerations, smacked of an ultimatum. Also, while the German government had already decided upon a postponement, Hoover pre-empted its declaration, offering far more than the Germans had expected to receive. Since the moratorium was a gift, not a concession triumphantly wrested from the foe, Brüning gained no political advantage from it. Finally, while Hoover's proposal offered much relief to British and American private investors and to the German government, it provided no consolation to France, who would lose substantially more than she would gain. Predictably, France protested, pointing out that Germany's problem was credit, not reparations, and arguing that, since Germany's budget was virtually balanced (unlike that of most European countries) even with reparations, she surely could pay the unconditional portion of the Young annuities. The British Treasury conceded that this was so (and in fact Germany had expected to pay that much) but insisted that nothing less than a full moratorium would satisfy panicky private investors.[15]

Frantic Franco-American negotiations ensued. As the Americans had little experience in the intricacies of reparations, they relied heavily on British experts for advice. While French leaders accepted the inevitability of the Hoover moratorium, they angled for German political concessions, especially the abandonment of Cruiser B and the customs union, but to no avail. The French government was also determined to retain at least a paper fiction of partial payment, partly for political reasons and partly out of realisation that once reparations were entirely halted, they would never resume, although the debts to America which they were designed to cover would remain to be paid. After much debate the American negotiators agreed that Germany technically would pay unconditional annuities to the Bank for International Settlements while actually receiving most or all of them back as a reloan. But Germany refused this arrangement, so, in the end, Germany paid the money to herself, but the fiction of reparations payments was precariously maintained. Thus the Hoover moratorium went into effect on 6 July. When news of final agreement reached Washington the French ambassador called for champagne and offered the prophetic toast: 'To the crisis we have just avoided and to the catastrophe which will follow.'[16]

Catastrophe came swiftly. While much of the Hoover year was consumed by debate over what to do when it ended, at first there was no time to think ahead. The moratorium came too late to salvage German credit, especially since futile British efforts toward all-around cancellation of debts and reparations only aggravated the German situation. By mid-July failure of a major German firm endangering two large banks had set off an unequalled financial panic generating a new flight from the mark and massive withdrawals of short-term credits, together with forced closure of all German banks for two days, permanent collapse of one very large bank, and closure of the German Stock Exchange for two months. The credit crisis continued to mount while the German standstill led to bank failures and closures all over central Europe along with a sharp withdrawal of foreign funds from London. Britain could not advance additional credits and France would not consider a long-term loan without an equally long-term political moratorium. But Brüning, continually faced with Nazi pressure, refused to affirm the political *status quo*. Further American loans were not forthcoming as Germany refused to restrict the flight of capital and the Federal Reserve thus saw no future in pouring endless funds into a leaky vessel.

At this juncture, Germany entered upon government by presidential decree without hope of return. Through the emergency presidential powers, Brüning imposed restriction after unpopular restriction upon the suffering German people, cutting wages, centralising government in a Cabinet without political support, and regimenting the economy to a degree rivalling that of totalitarian Russia, thus unintentionally laying the groundwork for the Hitlerian transformation to come. Cutting prices and wages inevitably deepened the German depression as firms failed and unemployment mounted. However, while most governments were unwilling to risk the untried tactics of deficit spending, public works, and inflationary policies, the German government could not in any circumstances do so. Domestically, memories of the 1923 inflation only eight years before were too harrowing to render such a course feasible, while internationally the imperatives of German credit rendered it equally impossible.

In short order, the German situation became so critical that the Bank for International Settlements was asked to appoint a Banker's Committee representing central banks to recommend some solution. In mid-August it produced an ambivalent report, offending nobody but providing no clear-cut guidance, primarily because financial remedies depended on major political decisions which few countries were willing to face.[17] By this time, too, attention had shifted to London, where withdrawal of foreign credits had reached panic proportions as a consequence of depression-generated budget deficits, unfavourable trade balances, and heavy British loans to other beleaguered nations. Many of these loans were being frozen in a well-intentioned effort to prevent further deterioration in central Europe. As speculation against the pound mounted emergency credits on 1 August from the Bank of France and the Federal Reserve failed to stem the tide. By 26 August they had largely evaporated as withdrawals continued. Since additional credits were not forthcoming without excruciatingly unpopular financial stringencies, the Labour Cabinet resigned, to be replaced by a three-party emergency National Government with MacDonald continuing as Prime Minister and Lord Reading, a Liberal, as Foreign Minister. In November he was replaced by another Liberal, Sir John Simon, after an election had confirmed the national coalition in office.

Annus terribilis took a heavy toll of the world's political leadership. Russia's closed and regimented economy moved serenely on, impervious to free-market fluctuations, leading many unemployed young western intellectuals to conclude that while capitalism was dying, communism was the wave of the future. Of the major western countries France weathered the crisis least agonisingly with her strongly restored currency, evenly balanced economy, and relatively lesser dependence on the sharply contracting international market. Even so, the increasingly aged and enfeebled Briand, while lingering on at the Quai d'Orsay, was severely weakened politically and lost the presidential election of 1931 as a consequence of the customs union proposal. Curtius, too, was a victim of the customs union project, and Brüning became his own Foreign Minister when it was abandoned. In the industrial countries, large and small, human misery was extreme, and governments correspondingly precarious. In far-off Japan the moderate ministry was losing its grip. And in 1932 the depression was to claim among its victims Brüning, Hoover, and the Herriot ministry in France, which fell in December when it attempted payment on the American debt.

When the first of the new depression-generated governments, the British national coalition, took office in late August 1931, it faced acute financial emergency. Additional French and American credits provided a brief respite, but speculative pressure on the pound soon resumed. As Paris and New York could no longer afford massive credits, on 21 September the new government took the drastic step of abandoning the Gold Standard. Henceforth the pound sterling would no longer be freely convertible to gold at a fixed rate. In effect the pound was devalued in relation to other currencies to stop the panic and to stimulate exports by lowering the price of British goods abroad. While devaluation did not work an instant cure for Britain's adverse trade balance of imports over exports, it did stem the London panic, but only at the cost of a new collapse in stock prices on the continent, in America, and in Japan. In Germany the Stock Exchange closed again on the day of British devaluation and remained closed for nearly seven months. Everywhere interest rates soared, firms failed, unemployment mounted, and *annus terribilis* became more terrible as a chain reaction forced country after country to abandon or suspend the Gold Standard. Others, including France and Italy, responded to the British devaluation by erecting high tariff barriers against potential

British dumping of low-priced goods on their sickly markets. International trade contracted still further, and everywhere the depression worsened, bringing more bank failures, more corporate failures, more unemployment, and more stock-market collapses. The depression fed upon itself as every disaster in the interlocking industrial, commercial, and financial world immediately generated many more, both within a given country and in the furthest reaches of the globe, demonstrating the horrifying interrelatedness of absolutely everything.

The reason why the depression was so universal and so severe was that, in the twentieth century, the world's financial structure had become entirely interlocking. In the eighteenth century the French government could reach virtual bankruptcy without Japan even knowing about it, much less being affected, but no longer. Late nineteenth-century imperialism, political and economic, had knit the world together. Now Britain and America were the two world-wide financial powers. Of these Britain had colonies and investments all over the globe and was heavily dependent on world trade. But she had spent her treasure in the First World War, remained in precarious economic and financial condition throughout the twenties, and was immediately sensitive to economic contractions in America both directly and through reactions in central Europe, where the Bank of England was deeply committed financially. America had also become heavily involved in world trade as she acquired an empire and sought markets for her endless bounty abroad. More importantly America, who emerged from the First World War with her abundant wealth intact and no war debts to mention,* had now become the world's banker, everybody's source of investment capital and governmental loans. A precarious world-wide financial structure based on unsecured short-term loans had developed. As long as investor confidence remained unshaken and loans were not recalled, all was well, but when panic set in on Wall Street, Britain's problems immediately multiplied. As the loss of confidence soon became universal, the chain reaction of disaster rapidly became global. The catastrophe was so unprecedented that nobody knew what to do.

Before anybody could do anything, war broke out in the Far

---

* America quickly and easily paid off her domestic war debt. Throughout the twenties, government budgets were small and balanced, and the dollar was unassailable.

War in China 1930 actually 1926

East. The new crisis exacerbated the old as the Tokyo stock exchange reacted violently, adding to the woes of other nations, particularly those several western countries with substantial investments in Japan or China, the other party to the conflict. Here, by 1930, Chiang Kai-shek had become the dominant figure and had succeeded in gaining control of much of China, including the allegiance of the local Manchurian warlord but none the less Nationalist control of this northernmost region was nominal. In 1931, as the Chinese civil war resumed, control became even more ephemeral. Japan held treaty rights dating from 1915 in Manchuria, including control of the South Manchurian Railway. On 18 September 1931 an explosion on the railway north of Mukden served as a pretext for skirmishes between Japanese troops guarding the railway and nearby Chinese forces, and for the enlargement of Japanese military activity thereafter toward the conquest of Manchuria.

The hostilities in Manchuria had been set off by local Japanese forces without the consent of either the Japanese government or the General Staff in Tokyo. As the Japanese troops advanced, meeting little resistance, they were not to be denied, and the progressively more feeble civilian government in Tokyo quickly lost any effective control over the situation. In both China and Japan the pressures of public opinion quickly escalated the affair into a major conflict, even creating a certain brief semblance of unity in China.

On 21 September the Chinese Nationalist government appealed to the United States under the Kellogg–Briand Pact and to the League under Article 11 of the Covenant, which did not automatically require League action.[18] At the behest of western leaders, who wanted to minimise both the conflict and League responsibility to act, the Chinese Nationalist government refrained from citing Articles 10 and 16, which would have required League action against Japan, refrained also from a declaration of war, and made no military resistance. In consequence Chiang was severely criticised for failure to defend nominally Chinese territories, and much was made of the fact that since neither party had declared war, no legal state of war existed.

The outbreak of hostilities and the consequent Chinese appeal caused much confusion at Geneva. The depression had so thoroughly dominated all thought and action that the world of diplomacy was taken by surprise. Little reliable information was available about actual conditions in Manchuria and, given the slowness of communication then from that remote spot, little more was available for weeks to come. As there was a universal disinclination to act, much emphasis was placed on China's lack of control in Manchuria, on Japan's treaty right to station troops there, and on the argument that therefore events in Manchuria did not constitute the invasion of one sovereign state by another. On 30 September the League Council passed an empty resolution and adjourned, hoping that the situation would resolve itself. Meanwhile Japanese military advances continued.

Armed with the advantage of hindsight and possibly with a pro-western bias, history has condemned Japan for the conquest of Manchuria. At the time, however, western opinion was divided, with substantial sympathy for Japan as the representative of the civilised west in the barbarous east. As the ancient Chinese culture was non-western, it was thought at best quaint and at worst primitive. The Chinese economy was indeed chaotic and the political situation turbulent, so much so that some doubted whether China constituted a sovereign state within the meaning of the Covenant. Throughout the twenties, rising Chinese nationalism had taken the form of anti-foreign demonstrations and efforts to end the extra-territorial privileges of foreign colonies there, thus evoking considerable hostility from western powers determined to hold what they had. Japan on the other hand had westernised with frenetic haste in the late nineteenth century to escape China's fate. Her law codes, government structure, industrial organisation, and armed forces all imitated western models. Her economy was sophisticated, her country apparently united, and her ministry moderate. In short, she was a 'civilised' nation to which many western powers had close economic ties.

Even if the undoubted fact that Japan was engaged in conquering Manchuria was faced, what could be done? The League could hardly uphold Japan's action. Neither could it condemn or expel her, as Japan would veto motions to such ends. Even the lesser act of sending a commission of inquiry might inflame Japanese nationalism and doom the moderate ministry, whose lack of control was not widely recognised. Idealists talked of the force of world opinion, but it had no force as opinion was divided and Japan, where the war was immensely popular, was indifferent to it. Realists recognised that only military force could stop Japan, but who would supply it? For most countries the League's concept o collective security rested upon an assumption that somebody else would supply the security. In fact keeping the peace depended, as always, upon the great powers. However, even in Britain, the major power where popular support for the League was strongest, the ordinary citizen assumed that other countries would do the shooting, should matters ever come to that. In no country was there much popular support for military action against Japan and no government seriously considered it. In fact the only League members with the remotest prospect of action were Britain and France and, in reality, neither could act. After years of budget slashing, shrinking armies, and naval disarmament, neither had the military power to embark on a course which, in any event, would probably bring down their depression-burdened governments and invite Japanese retaliation against their trade and their Asian colonies.

The other two powers with the theoretical possibility of action were not members of the League. Russia remained warily neutral, as she was preoccupied with European and domestic problems and unprepared for an Asian war. While denouncing Japanese imperialism, the Soviet Union even-handedly remarked that it differed little from western imperialism in China.[19] Britain quietly echoed this sentiment in other terms, noting that in view of her own actions at Shanghai in 1927, she could hardly condemn Japan.

As those few who sought action looked for somebody else to take it, the last remaining somebody was the United States. In America the prevailing mood was overwhelmingly isolationist, racist, hostile to the League, and preoccupied with the depression. Neither Chinese nor Japanese were very popular after decades of talk about the 'yellow peril'. Within the government there was a clear comprehension of military inadequacy to take action, as America also was largely disarmed, but relatively little awareness of the possibility of future Japanese-American conflict in the Pacitfic. While government counsels were divided, there was a general inclination to let the League take the lead. Like everybody else, America said, 'After you'.

In the circumstances it is not surprising that nothing was done. Disarmament, disunity, depression, and public indifference had rendered impossible any collective action against open aggression by a major power, if indeed it ever had been possible. The League, unable to evade the issue altogether, assiduously avoided action of any variety and limited itself to hollow phraseology. As Japan bombed Manchurian towns, China gained a special session of the League Council in mid-October with an American observer actually in attendance. The Council passed a resolution urging Japanese withdrawal within three weeks, which was not binding as Japan voted against it, and adjourned until mid-November. In Manchuria the Japanese troops marched on, undeterred by an increasingly chaotic China or by political and economic upheavals in Japan.

When the Council met in November Japan rejected Chinese offers of arbitration or judicial settlement. In secret sessions accompanied by small-power protests and further Japanese advances in Manchuria, Britain strenuously opposed economic sanctions, knowing by then that America would not participate and that sanctions could thus accomplish little except Japanese retaliation against Britain's battered trade balance. Finally, in open sessions on 9 and 10 December, the Council again called for Japanese withdrawal but without a time limit. Japan could, however, pursue 'bandits', a loophole affording ample excuse for further military activity. The League also authorised a five-man commission representing the four major European powers and America, with Chinese and Japanese assessors attached, to investigate on the spot. Thereupon it adjourned, able to delay any further action until the commission's report was received.

The commission, under the leadership of Lord Lytton of Britain, embarked on a slow journey across the Atlantic, across America, and across the Pacific, reaching Tokyo more than two months later on 29 February 1932. By then Japan had gained effective control of Manchuria, and on 9 March the puppet state of Manchukuo was established under Japanese auspices. In anticipation of either a puppet state or outright annexation, America had in January proclaimed Stimson's doctrine of non-recognition of the legality of either the *de facto* situation or any treaty arising from it.[20] While this declaration aided China not one whit, it was the first moral condemnation of Japanese aggression. The other powers remained silent. In January, too, Japanese forces at Shanghai's International Settlement became involved in conflict with the Chinese and fighting continued for more than a month. Stimson had wanted to warn Japan away from Shanghai and to reinforce the Anglo-American contingents there, but the British refused. As the fighting continued, Stimson favoured naval demonstrations at a safe distance and appeal to the 1922 Nine Power Pact, but Britain, torn between offending Japan and offending America, waffled and wavered, so nothing was done. By early March a ceasefire was in effect in Shanghai and the Japanese soon began to withdraw.

Throughout the months the League waited to hear from Lord Lytton, while small powers with a vested interest in maintaining the League's viability and no risk of direct involvement themselves protested major power inaction. Their efforts led the Assembly on 11 March to salvage its honour by endorsing non-recognition. While this would not save Manchuria, the great powers would not go further as each was preoccupied with the depression and domestic politics. Britain, further preoccupied with Empire and the forthcoming Ottawa Conference, was increasingly hostile to Japan but unwilling to act without France and America. In both countries forthcoming elections ruled out any action, while Britain and America remained convinced that they lacked the military capacity to act. Thus the powers pursued a very limited policy with even more limited results.

While Japan was mopping up Manchuria, the Disarmament Conference opened at Geneva on 2 February 1932. The mistiming was typical of its entire history. Among the fifty-nine delegations the conference's saddest figure was its chairman and only true believer, Arthur Henderson, the former British Labour Foreign Secretary.[21] If one man's will could have made the conference a success, it would have been. Henderson had devoted much of his life to disarmament and regarded the conference as the pinnacle of his career. His superhuman efforts were unavailing and he was a broken man when the conference ended, dying soon thereafter. The failure of the conference was fore-ordained. Most delegates recognised that the time was not ripe for disarmament, what with battleships abuilding in Germany, sabres rattling in Italy, bombs bursting in Manchuria, and rearmament in progress in Russia and also in France to a degree. Furthermore, almost inevitably, 'The Germans demanded payment in the coin of French and Polish disarmament; the French in the coin of British and American commitments; the British in the coin of French disarmament and American commitments – and so on through the whole catalogue of sovereign self-centred nations.'[22]

Beyond that, the irreducible problem dominating the several intermittent sessions of the conference through 1932 and 1933 was that Germany demanded equality while France insisted upon security, but if Germany gained equality, France had no security since Germany was larger and fundamentally stronger. Repeatedly Germany argued that other powers should disarm to her level (i.e. Versailles Treaty limits as adapted to the relative strength of the countries concerned) or variously that she should be allowed to rearm without restriction. A fear-driven France with an inherently weaker power-base and broader commitments could accept neither argument. There was much 'public pronouncing and private conversing'[23] and frequent adjournments when deadlock was reached. When meetings resumed after more private diplomacy, one delegation or another, often that of Britain, would present an elaborately worded scheme to paper over the divide. Proposal after proposal foundered on the sharp rock of irreconcilable conflict between German equality and French security.[24]

Throughout the interminable disarmament debates, Brüning and his successors argued that concessions must be made to Germany to prevent the accession of Hitler to power. Indeed this had been Brüning's tactic ever since September 1930. There is no evidence to suggest that additional concessions would have had the slightest effect beyond generating demands for even more, but in 1932 events in Germany seemed to give some force to the argument, for the Hitlerian tide was at the flood. Germany had four national elections in 1932: two presidential and two for the Reichstag, along with state and municipal elections. In all the Nazis did well. While Hindenburg was re-elected President, Hitler finished a solid second in both the initial round and the run-off, collecting eleven million votes. He was now established as the second man in Germany, and since the first was 85 years old and increasingly senile, Hitler was marked as the coming man. Brüning was responsible for Hindenburg's victory and so the Old Gentleman, with his customary gratitude, dismissed him on 30 May 1932, thus ending the last German ministry with a vestige of legitimacy. Brüning's successors, Franz von Papen and General Kurt von Schleicher, were unknown figures lacking any popular support. While foreign policy remained unchanged, particularly in demanding concessions to forestall Hitler, they governed exclusively by presidential decree, especially since the Nazis hit their peak in the

Hitler in Power

Reichstag elections of July 1932, taking 37 per cent of the vote, 230 seats, and the presidency of the Reichstag as the largest party. Undoubtedly the miseries of the depression sent many to the support of the man who vowed to break the Versailles *diktat* and rearm Germany. It was cold comfort to nervous neighbouring countries that in another Reichstag election in November, the Nazis lost a conspicuous number of seats. Their interior disarray and financial distress were not public knowledge, and the Nazis remained Germany's largest party.

Germany was not the only country to undergo political turbulence during 1932. Elsewhere the leadership was also aged, ailing, and failing. In Poland the elderly Pilsudski was increasingly enfeebled. In France Briand, frail and semi-senile, was forced from office by a cabinet crisis in January to that end.[25] He died in March, leaving only Chamberlain of the Locarno triumvirate alive but inactive. In the course of parliamentary elections early in May, which showed a swing to the left, the President of France was assassinated, causing an intense crisis and new presidential elections. Herriot succeeded in forming a ministry and survived in office until December. In Britain the elderly MacDonald continued in office but failing eyesight necessitated repeated surgery and inevitably a less-detailed direction of policy. His Foreign Secretary, Simon, was able but ambivalent, displaying great competence in the daily conduct of affairs but no clear commitment to any course of action. Across the Atlantic the November election repudiated Hoover as the depression worsened. In the four month hiatus before Franklin Roosevelt could be inaugurated, America ground to an economic standstill.

Throughout 1932 economic turbulence also continued unabated, even more widespread than political instability. Currencies tumbled and tariff walls rose. In the course of the year a universal tariff war developed as each country desperately tried to protect sinking domestic markets from foreign competition. Britain, who in 1931 had legislated her proudest interwar achievement, transformation of part of the British Empire into the British Commonwealth of Nations, complicated the tariff tangle by gaining at the Ottawa Conference of August 1932 an increase in imperial (or commonwealth) preference, the tariff reduction given among members of the British imperial family. This helped British exports but not those of countries outside the family, particularly since protectionist new duties were imposed against non-members. As the world economic situation deteriorated still further with normal trade channels entirely clogged and currencies completely unstable, some nations, Russia among them, reverted to primitive barter arrangements for exchange of goods without reference to money. In paralysed central Europe barter became commonplace.

As central Europe well demonstrated, one of the effects of the depression was to exacerbate existing problems, be they social, political, financial or ethnic. In hitherto stable Czechoslovakia where the German minority had largely come to accept and participate in the existing regime, the depression hurt the industrialised Germanic borderlands far more than the agricultural Bohemian plains. While the government took energetic relief measures, Germanic discontent swelled for Hitler to capitalise on later. Yugoslavia nearly shattered into its component parts as an Italian-supported Croatian revolt broke out in 1932. Even western Europe showed ethnic strains as tension in otherwise peaceful Belgium mounted between Flemings and Walloons. Austria was spared ethnic problems but had all others. A weak financial structure weakened further as Austria was the first country to collapse. Tension between the ruling conservative Catholic party and the socialists of Vienna intensified steadily. As in Czechoslovakia, local Nazis were preparing the future. In addition a right-wing nationalist *putsch* in September 1931 was suppressed at socialist insistence but the Catholic party remained in control of the government. Incidents between it and the Vienna socialists, along with Nazi-generated unrest, led to the abandonment of parliamentary democracy early in 1933 and the advent of government by decree.[26]

From one end of Europe to the other politics veered to the extremes of left and right. The trend was perhaps most marked in Spain where, having nudged its king into exile in 1931, the country suffered an alternating series of right-wing and left-wing governments, completely divided on matters social, religious and political, until the Spanish civil war of the late thirties settled the matter bloodily. In Germany not only Nazism but also communism gained adherents, and the two movements battled in the streets. As there were so many unemployed, there were plenty to fight. In Bulgaria there was a sharp swing to the left, not only nationally but in the Sofia municipal elections, which the Communists won in 1932. Greek politics entered a state of total flux with acute tension between

the rising royalists and ebbing republicans. The failure of republi-
can *coups* in 1933 and 1935 led finally to restoration of the monarchy
and soon to dictatorship.

Dictatorship did seem the only solution to the social and political
pressures generated by the depression, especially in countries lacking a long tradition of political stability. Stalin had no unrest to
contend with. Nor did Pilsudski and Mussolini. While both countries suffered economically and Italy was nearly forced off the gold
standard, dictatorship ensured political and social stability.
Romania and Yugoslavia went into royal dictatorship in 1931. In
Hungary a financial collapse caused by the Austrian banking crisis
led to League intervention, unpopular financial stringencies, and
Fascist dictatorship in 1932. Other countries took a little longer to
reap the whirlwind. For some, the harvest did not come home until
the Second World War. But misery was universal in 1932, and
everywhere most people hoped to alleviate their distress at the
expense of some other social, political, or ethnic entity. This fact
had been evident during meetings in London in August 1931 to
work out some of the technicalities of the Hoover moratorium and
became increasingly apparent as the end of the Hoover year
neared.

Through the mounting distress of 1932, while harried Cabinets
coped with the immediate political, economic, and social problems,
they had another constant worry: what to do when the Hoover
moratorium expired on 1 July? As Hoover could take no further
initiative in a presidential election year, especially in view of
intense Congressional hostility to debt cancellation, reparations
and war-debt payments would resume unless some solution were
found. Of necessity Hoover left it to the European powers. It was
fairly widely recognised that neither Germany nor her creditors
were in fit condition to pay what they owed. German governments
insisted that sweeping concessions, preferably cancellation, were as
essential in reparations as in disarmament, both for financial reasons
and to halt Hitler. Germany's hard-pressed creditors, several of
them fearful for their security, were reluctant to see the end of
reparations or to abandon any prospect of their own financial
relief, particularly since war debts would remain to be paid, whatever happened to reparations. They tended to argue that if Germany could afford to rearm, she could afford to pay reparations.
France sought a German political moratorium regarding the Polish

Corridor in particular and modification of the Versailles Treaty in general in return for a cancellation which she was reluctant to make but increasingly recognised to be inevitable. Germany, knowing also that cancellation was inevitable, held firm against endorsement of the political *status quo* and, as negotiations progressed, pointed to her electoral returns.

The inevitability of some form of cancellation heightened as an intense Congressional reaction prevented extension of the Hoover moratorium and British financial circles threw their weight behind outright cancellation. Then another special committee of the Bank for International Settlements, convened under clauses of the Young Plan concerning postponement of German annuities, reported in late December 1931 that postponement of the conditional annuities would be appropriate but entirely inadequate. The committee hinted in the broadest terms at the necessity for all-around cancellation of reparations and war debts to hasten economic recovery.[27]

Britain immediately summoned a conference of the Young Plan countries at Lausanne in early January 1932. It was postponed first by an extended French political crisis, then by French and German elections, and finally by lack of agreement on what to do. Britain, Germany, and Italy wanted full cancellation of reparations; France did not. She was willing to reduce reparations to the extent that her debts were reduced and to be accommodating about modes of payment, but not to forego the net profit which the reparations–debts cycle yielded to her under the Young Plan. As Britain, Germany and America all had serious credit problems, they wished to give priority to private debts over public. France had nothing to gain but much to lose from such a move, but much to gain from a united Anglo-French front against America on the debt question. Britain refused that. As each country sought maximum advantage, there was much Anglo-French discussion of an all-European moratorium on reparations and debts, leaving the American question for post-election resolution. Britain and France could not agree on its duration, while Germany abruptly declared that no moratorium of any length was acceptable.[28] Only outright cancellation in full would, in German eyes, restore the German economy and financial structure. While the absolute conjunction between reparations and the German financial crisis was absurd over-simplification, it was widely believed by the German citizenry, and, not surprisingly, the German government adhered without deviation to this line.

The end of the Hoover year was approaching. Accordingly, while little was agreed, Britain and France drafted a masterly invitation, which carefully avoided all mention of either reparations or war debts, for a conference at Lausanne in mid-June to effect a 'lasting settlement'.[29] By the time that it met, the disarmament conference was nearing the end of its first long dreary session, which adjourned on 23 July. Two simultaneous huge conferences strained diplomatic resources to the limit as skeleton staffs tended Foreign Ministries at home while harried statesmen shuttled from Geneva to Lausanne. When Germany recognised that full cancellation was not obtainable, she tried to link the two conferences, demanding full rearmament as the price for one final token reparations payment.

When the Lausanne Conference convened on 16 June with MacDonald presiding, it first suspended German reparations and inter-Allied non-American debt payments for the duration of the conference, thus obviating the need to finish before 1 July. It also agreed to hold the American problem in abeyance until the European one was solved. Then agreement ceased. It took all of MacDonald's genial skill as chairman to keep the conference from complete collapse. In the end agreement was reached only because the sole alternative of reversion to the Young Plan was out of the question. Accordingly several misleading documents were finally initialled on 9 July.[30]

Under the Lausanne Convention Germany was to make a final lump-sum payment of three milliard marks in government bonds to the Bank for International Settlements immediately after the Convention was ratified and went into force. After a three-year moratorium, the Bank could market the bonds if German financial conditions permitted. As the Lausanne Convention was never ratified, the bonds were never transferred. That this prospect had been considered is evident in the fact that allocation of the three milliard was left for later decision and in the signature by the four principal recipients of a 'Gentleman's Agreement' that they would not ratify the Convention until war-debt relief was obtained from America. It was further agreed that the moratorium on inter-allied debts and German payments would continue until the Lausanne Convention went into effect, cancelling the reparations clauses of the Young Plan and Hague Agreements. Subsidiary documents extended the moratorium on non-German reparations until December and established a committee to work out a solution in the interim, established another committee to tackle the financial and economic reconstruction of central and eastern Europe, and issued a call for a world economic and monetary conference to seek solutions to the world crisis.*

Thus ended reparations. The Lausanne Agreements sparked much resentment in Germany, where full cancellation had been anticipated as an absolute right. Since the Gentleman's Agreement soon became public knowledge, it was obvious that the final payment was merely a paper fiction, a sop to French opinion, but Germany was insulted and the results showed in the July election returns. The Gentleman's Agreement called in effect for another conference if the Lausanne Convention failed of ratification, but it was never held as reparations were overtaken by events and the futility of inviting Hitler to discuss payment was evident to all. Reparations quietly fell into limbo, a victim of German revisionism and world depression. Over the years from the Armistice to the Hoover moratorium, Germany had paid a little more than twenty milliard marks, slightly over the amount she was committed by the Versailles Treaty to pay by 1 May 1921.[31] This not very grand total included credits for transferred properties and deliveries in kind under the Versailles Treaty and all subsequent reparations plans. Hungary and Bulgaria had paid some reparations, mostly in properties ceded, but not much. Turkey and Austria had effectively paid nothing at all. The entire tangled history of reparations demonstrated the futility of imposing large indemnities on destitute or powerful nations. The smaller states could not pay and Germany would not. While it is arguable whether Germany could have entirely fulfilled the 50 milliard marks of the original London Schedule of Payments, she undoubtedly could have paid more than she did, had she seen any reason to do so. But as she chose not to pay, she won in the end at tremendous cost to herself and others. Reparations generated a huge bureaucracy, endless conferences, intense ill-will in most of the countries concerned, and unprecedented difficulties in European money markets, all for very little.

* When the World Economic Conference finally met in June 1933, its efforts at currency stabilisation were torpedoed by President Roosevelt's refusal to co-operate. Thereafter it died a lingering death.

In the end they contributed to and complicated the great depression, but their concealed demise did nothing to alleviate the economic crisis.

Although reparations were laid to rest, war debts to America were not. In December some governments managed to scrape up their payments while others defaulted. In France the Herriot government fell over the issue. In 1933 everybody defaulted except three non-European countries and Finland, each with small debts and correspondingly minuscule payments, which continued regularly. War debts to America contracted during the First World War were never cancelled, and the United States Treasury still computes the amounts owed, which have multiplied as interest has compounded.[32]

While the European powers were struggling toward a reparations settlement in the spring and summer of 1932, they put far-away Manchuria out of mind, but the Lytton Commission was hard at work investigating the situation in Japan, Manchuria and China. Its unanimous report was signed in Peking on 4 September and shipped to Geneva via the trans-Siberian railway, arriving too late for the Assembly meeting in mid-September. When the contents of the report became known in early October, there was dismay in Geneva. By then most countries had accepted the *fait accompli* in Manchuria and hoped that time would bury the matter. The Lytton Report[33] did not accelerate that process.

While the all-western Lytton Commission praised Japanese westernisation, criticised Chinese lack of it, and lauded Japanese contributions to Manchuria's economic development, it sustained China on the essential points. The Commission judged that Japan was responsible for the puppet regime, which lacked any local Chinese support. The report recommended its removal, restoration of Chinese sovereignty, and autonomy for Manchuria, along with numerous foreign advisers, many of them Japanese. The League Council met in late November to consider these unwelcome proposals and promptly passed the problem on to the Assembly, which met in early December. There some of the small states urged condemnation of Japan while the major powers stressed 'complexities' and 'conciliation'.[34] As agreement seemed impossible, a committee was charged with seeking one. It devoted the next two months to a hopeless task.

Yet still the Far Eastern crisis, like the continuing disarmament deadlock, would not subside quietly. On 1 January 1933 after another suspicious railway incident, Japanese forces crossed the Chinese frontier into the province of Jehol, which Japan claimed was part of Manchuria. Japanese troops progressed easily, generating much western scorn at Chinese weakness and taking the provincial capital on 4 March. By that time the League Assembly had on 24 February 1933, in the face of renewed Japanese aggression, finally adopted the Lytton Report, with forty-two states voting for it, Japan voting against it, and Siam abstaining. The Japanese delegation left the hall. In March they left Geneva altogether as Japan formally withdrew from the League, the first great power to do so.

Meanwhile the depression deepened again and the disarmament disputes dragged on, with German representatives rarely in attendance. But by now the squabbles of Geneva had been overshadowed by events elsewhere, and European eyes turned to Berlin, where on 30 January 1933 Adolf Hitler became the last Chancellor of the Weimar Republic. That long-dreaded event had finally occurred and, in the months to come, the Hitlerian transformation of the Weimar Republic into the totalitarian Third Reich dominated diplomatic concern, especially in neighbouring countries but throughout Europe as well, as each nation sought to assess what the new situation meant for it. Few of Europe's leaders had any illusions that the change boded better times ahead. The three years past had destroyed optimism and drained hope almost to the dregs.

6 The End of All Illusion

I⊤ has been commonplace to assume that most western leaders
were slow to recognise what Hitler's accession to power meant. One
is often told that there was considerable relief that Germany's
political turbulence had ended and that finally Germany had a
government which could command a majority in the Reichstag,
along with widespread hope that power would tame Hitler and that
he really did not mean what he said. Such notions were common
and perhaps entirely understandable but they were rarely to be
found in the ministries of European governments. Needless to say,
nobody envisaged the holocaust* ahead and it appears that most
western diplomatists misjudged Hitler's intentions towards Poland,
thinking that like his predecessors he sought frontier revision, when
in fact he viewed Poland only as an entity to be destroyed *en route* to
Russia.[1] But on the main issue there was, especially at first, little
illusion. Most of Europe's leaders realised that Nazism was a threat
to Europe's peace and that in the long run Hitler intended war. In
April 1933 Herriot told an American visitor, 'we shall have to fight
them again'.[2]

Such illusions as existed tended to arise from desperation and
were nourished by Hitler's early diplomatic caution. As he had
insisted upon coming to power legally rather than by a putsch, so
also was he Adolf *légalité* in foreign affairs until he had established
his total control in Germany and multiplied the military instruments
at his command. In October 1933 Hitler withdrew Germany from
the moribund Disarmament Conference and from the League,
dismaying but not astounding most diplomatists. None the less, he
continued to speak the language of Geneva. It suited Hitler to talk
of peace while he prepared to wage war.

Among those who were not deceived by Hitler's protestations of

* A term signifying wholesale destruction or, more specifically, Hitler's
systematic extermination of about six million European Jews during the
Second World War.

peaceful intentions was Stalin. Anti-imperialist propaganda ceased abruptly and Litvinov remained Foreign Minister while Hitler put his antisemitic creed increasingly into practice in Germany. In September 1934 Russia joined the League of Nations, which she had for so long denounced, and Litvinov soon became Geneva's leading apostle of collective security. Security against whom? That question did not need to be asked, particularly when Russia entered into military alliances with Czechoslovakia and France in 1935.

Czechoslovakia felt the force of Nazi propaganda in her large German minority at once.[3] She not only reinforced her security by the alliance with Russia but also moved to strengthen the Little Entente into a formal organisation with a permanent structure. Moves to this end had begun in 1929 in response to Mussolini's attempt to dominate Danubia, but the organisation envisaged then and in 1932 planning sessions had become far more extensive by 1933, including regular general-staff consultations, partly in response to the advent of Hitler.[4] The new organisation did immediate and successful battle in 1933 against Mussolini's proposal for a Four Power Pact.

This proposal was Mussolini's own reaction to Hitler's accession. While relieved that Hitler displayed no concern for the Germanic south Tyrol, Mussolini was alarmed by Hitler's obvious interest in Austria. Therefore Mussolini not only sought to strengthen his own diplomatic position by a plan to revive a great-power Concert of Europe but also, by proposing territorial revisions, to distract Hitler from the Danube and appease him at the expense of Poland. This blatant ploy drew immediate response from the equally threatened Little Entente. France could hardly jettison all her eastern allies at once and so declined to sign Mussolini's document until it was diluted to the point of meaninglessness. Hitler himself had no interest in the Polish corridor and much disliked multilateral pacts, preferring bilateral treaties as easier to break when the time came. He too signed the Four Power Pact, the sole multilateral arrangement he ever accepted, only when it had been thoroughly emasculated.[5]

Poland was nearly paralysed with fear. Under the leadership of the failing Pilsudski, she came to terms with Hitler and signed a Polish–German Non-aggression Declaration in January 1934 to match the similar treaty with Russia signed in July 1932.[6] What else to do? To seek any real refuge in Russia's arms was unthinkable.

Thereafter Poland, whose chief concerns were peace and the *status quo*, tried to maintain a precarious balance between her two dangerous neighbours. The tension eased temporarily as Hitler chose to placate Poland while he prepared to devour her, but the Franco-Russian alliance raised new fears of domination from the other direction. Poland's dilemma of equal perils from east and west engendered continuing paralysis until the German and Russian armies simultaneously invaded her in 1939. To the south, Austria was similarly paralysed, especially after the abortive Nazi *coup* in Vienna in 1934. On that occasion Mussolini massed troops on the Brenner Pass. Thereafter a frightened Austria, increasingly torn by domestic dissension, placed its hopes in Italian protection, which steadily ebbed as Hitler courted Mussolini.

In the west paralysis set in to a degree in Belgium as well but it took a little longer. Like France Belgium pressed on with new vigour to complete her frontier fortifications and, unlike France, proceeded to rearm regardless of budget deficits, assuming another war to be inevitable. Belgium also wasted no time in seeking a British guarantee. As early as February 1933, the Belgian Foreign Ministry began a series of efforts to this end. With their failure Belgium displayed a certain fatalism along with growing fear that French commitments in eastern Europe, especially the Russian tie, would drag Belgium into an unwanted war with Germany. As a consequence, Belgian policy became increasingly ostrich-like.[7]

In France, too, the initial reaction was swift. In March 1933 the French Premier and Foreign Minister were startlingly forthright and detailed in spelling out the danger to their British counterparts.[8] France pressed on with efforts already begun to complete the Maginot Line quickly, rebuild her navy, and reorganise her air force, but rearmament was slowed by the knowledge of a succession of weak cabinets that deficit financing could not carry the Chamber. As additional security was imperative, Louis Barthou, a man of no illusions, moved in 1934 toward an eastern Locarno and, with its predictable failure, on toward the alliance with Russia, despite Polish dismay. But with his accidental assassination in October 1934 on the occasion of a state visit by King Alexander of Yugoslavia, the momentum slackened. As early as 1933 French leaders believed that Germany had already achieved numerical military superiority.[9] With continuing evidence of German rearmament and Hitlerian belligerance, especially the 1934 attempt on Austria and Hitler's announcement in March 1935 of open rearmament, France became increasingly frightened. But the country was riven by particularly divisive political scandals in 1934, and thereafter there was no agreement whatever on how to face the external threat. Instead a bitter ideological battle was fought over whether to join Russia against Germany, to join Germany against Russia, or to stand fast against Germany without contaminating oneself by association with communism. The disunity caused a paralysis of the will all too evident in 1936 when Hitler remilitarised the Rhineland, repudiating the Locarno pacts in the process, and put his army on France's frontier.

In Britain as in France many people were reluctant to draw close either to communism or to Nazism. They tended to hope that Russia and Germany would fight each other, destroy each other, and thus conveniently resolve the problem. The Foreign Office was less sanguine. The Hitlerian menace was recognised at once, but the instinct was to temporise, especially with Simon at the helm, while exhorting France to rearm. In January 1933 the British were delighted that the new French Air Minister was committed to disarmament. Their tune soon changed as they urged France to shoulder the burden but refused joint staff talks.[10] The traditional British disinclination to become committed on the continent was combined with growing awareness of the extreme inadequacy of Britain's military forces. In March 1932, partly in response to the Manchurian conflict, Britain tacitly abandoned her long-standing blithe assumption that no war need be expected for ten years and formally abolished this obsolete policy guideline in late 1933 in the wake of Hitler's advent.[11] Thereafter Britain rearmed as quickly as was politically feasible – but that was very slowly. In 1935 all three parties, sensing the prevailing mood, fought the general election on the incongruous platform of disarmament and collective security. Winston Churchill was in the political wilderness partly because he called for rearmament. The British people put their faith in collective security to be provided by somebody else and managed to believe, because they wanted to believe, that an enfeebled and discredited League, once its members were thoroughly disarmed, could stop aggression by its most powerful and belligerent member. When the election was safely past the new Conservative government began quiet rearmament, but such a process, especially when quiet, requires much time.

While America had scant faith in the League, the situation was otherwise similar. The country was engulfed in depression and overwhelmingly preoccupied with domestic concerns. Isolationist sentiment was all-powerful, particularly since the Atlantic Ocean seemed a more adequate barrier than the English Channel. Roosevelt, whose inclinations were internationalist but whose political instincts were acute, effectively withdrew America from Europe altogether in 1933 when he put domestic politics ahead of international economic co-operation, indicating that America was no more selfless than other states. While Roosevelt harboured no illusions about Hitler or about where America's interests lay, he was obliged to give primary attention to the domestic emergency and to hold foreign policy within the narrow limits prescribed by public opinion. As late as October 1937 Roosevelt tested the atmosphere with a speech proposing that international troublemakers be quarantined, but the reaction in America demonstrated that isolationism remained dominant. So also was pacifism. As the distance from Europe was greater, the American people insisted much longer than their British brethren upon beating their swords into ploughshares.

It is precisely because the western democracies were so slow to rearm that some have concluded that their leaders were slow to recognise the Hitlerian menace. On the contrary the slowness of rearmament arose from the fact that these countries were democracies. Dictators do not have to concern themselves with public opinion and, not surprisingly, Germany, Russia and Italy all rearmed rapidly. Japan, where the military men were increasingly dominant, did the same, and in 1937 invaded China, setting off the Second World War in the Far East. But in the western democracies such speedy rearmament was generally not possible. The depression, with its almost universal credo of budget-balancing and fiscal stringency, played a role in deferring heavy military expenditures, as did acute internal dissension in some countries. In the immediate years after Hitler's accession, Belgium could abandon financial orthodoxy in favour of deficit spending for rearmament because this country was united in its recognition of the threat and the appropriate response. An utterly divided France could not. But beyond these problems lay a deeper difficulty: the overwhelming commitment of western Europeans and Americans to peace and disarmament.

Public opinion rarely participates to any large degree in the formulation of foreign policy but it does set the outer limits of policy, especially when there is a strong tendency in any one direction. In the first years after Hitler's accession the limits were exceptionally narrow as popular enthusiasm for disarmament necessarily rendered impossible any policy with the slightest risk of force. Once public opinion is firmly set, it is usually slow to change unless an immediate and direct threat is perceived. Hitler was careful not to provide that threat for several years. In the interim the education of public opinion to a new view progressed, as always, very slowly except in some of Germany's immediate neighbours. And until public opinion shifted, there was no prospect that massive budgets for rearmament would be approved by parliaments, national assemblies, and congresses.

In part the western democracies were reaping the harvest of the disarmament conference. In 1931 in anticipation of its commencement and in hopes of ensuring its success, there had been an intense world-wide propaganda campaign in favour of disarmament. While this effort had no effect in Italy or Russia, its message took root most deeply in the English-speaking world where, in those days, it was needed least. In 1931 the Oxford Union, cradle of future British political leaders, debated and carried a resolution that 'this House will not fight for King and Country'. Across the Atlantic there was a widespread and growing belief that 'the munition makers were the merchants of death', a view soon reinforced by sensational public Congressional hearings on the armaments industry. In both countries peace movements were strong and becoming stronger.

Just as the Disarmament Conference opened in early 1932, Britain's leaders recognised the country's extreme military weakness and the need to educate the nation to the dangerous condition of the country's defences. However, they could hardly do so with disarmament hugely popular, the government officially committed to it, and a distinguished British statesman working desperately at Geneva to lead the nations to the light of disarmament and peace. Long before Hitler withdrew from the Disarmament Conference, French and British leaders realised that the deadlock could not be resolved and that nothing could be expected from the conference. Yet they did not know how to extricate themselves from it. Having just convinced the citizenry that disarmament was a sure and swift route to peace, and economical besides, they could hardly sound the tocsin, repudiate the conference, and demand expensive armaments. As no government wanted to incur the onus of killing the conference, it lingered on in diminished form into 1935, thus further postponing the re-education of Europe's idealists. Then came the 1935 British election, which no party wished to lose by telling the unpalatable truth.

In time Hitler provided enough direct and immediate threats to reverse public opinion, inevitably sooner in those countries close to Germany than in those more distant, but rarely soon enough. Most political leaders in the democracies were, whether by choice or by necessity, the prisoners of their electorates, and by the time those electorates faced up to the danger, the hour was late, particularly since modern weaponry cannot be created overnight. Through a number of crucial years, in the late twenties as well as the early thirties, the politicians had told the people what they wanted to hear and had led them to accept the illusion of peace rather than searching for the more elusive reality.

Throughout the interwar years there never existed any firm foundation for permanent peace since three of the four strongest continental powers were intensely dissatisfied with the *status quo*. Italy lacked the power to disturb the European peace to any substantial degree, but Russia and Germany were strong states, both steadily becoming stronger. As their strength grew so did their appetites, and they came to view the small nations on their borders as tempting morsels to be devoured at the first opportunity. Under the circumstances, the existing international structure lacked any aura of permanence.

It is a striking fact that, throughout the twenties and to a degree in the early thirties, both the statesmen and the ordinary peoples of Europe kept searching for a basis for permanent peace but never found it. Subconsciously they seemed aware that the existing structure lacked solid foundations and provided little security to anybody. As the interwar era brought the democratic experiment to areas where it had hitherto been unknown and the war had heightened the political consciousness of voters in western countries with longer democratic traditions, the statesmen could not ignore the deep-seated yearnings for peace of ordinary citizens. But as the statesmen could not build a stable peace on the foundation erected at Paris after the war, they fed their electorates on false hopes and pacified them with the illusion of peace. The camaraderie at Locarno and Thoiry, the solemn signing of the Kellogg–Briand Pact, and the soaring oratory of Geneva, vowing eternal dedication to the impossible dream of collective security, were all designed to reassure the nervous citizenry that the foundations of peace were firm. Over and over again, from 1920 through to 1930 and beyond, the peoples of Europe were told that true peace had come at last, but somehow, despite a natural inclination to swallow the hopeful illusion, they sensed that it had not, recognising that the situation was inherently volatile. Unfortunately as the threat to peace grew through the thirties, so also did the tendency to take refuge in illusion.

Clearly one of the leading characteristics of interwar Europe was instability of all varieties, political, economic, social and diplomatic. With rare exceptions such domestic political and social stability as European countries enjoyed arrived in the wake of dictatorship, as one central or east European country after another abandoned any effort to impose democracy on unprepared populations. Economically even the patchy prosperity of the late twenties rested on an impermanent and precarious base which shattered with startling suddenness. The fragile collective security afforded by the League of Nations proved to be similarly ephemeral. While small nations clung desperately, despite growing evidence to the contrary, to the hope that the League could save them from mighty and rapacious neighbours, the great powers devoted their oratory to concealing the fact that it could not and their energies to propping up a very fragile structure in hopes that its total collapse could be averted.

One of the several causes of instability in interwar Europe was the fact that the political fragmentation inherent in the postwar peace settlement was either too great or not great enough. No serious consideration was given after the First World War to the forcible break-up of Germany and Russia, as both would have required the sustained use of arms and prolonged occupation, prospects unattractive to the war-weary victors. On the other hand it was virtually impossible to revert to pre-war boundaries as the Habsburg Empire could not be reconstituted except by extended use of force, Poland could not be re-created without the transfer of some districts from Germany, and Communist Russia could not, given the prevailing climate of opinion, be allotted any more territory than the unavoidable minimum. And so the peacemakers chose a middle course, with all the dangers inherent in solutions which satisfied almost nobody and particularly dissatisfied those nations with the latent strength to alter the *status quo* in time. Clearly, the creation of a host of small, relatively weak states at the expense of great nations whose power had not been significantly reduced generated a potentially explosive situation. While the fuse proved to be twenty years long, it was evident from the outset that the *cordon sanitaire* was both fundamentally ineffectual in every sense and an invitation to German and Russian aggression once the time was ripe and the fuse had burnt down.

Another cause of instability was the fact that political fragmentation necessitated a compensatory economic integration which did not occur. Indeed ancient hostilities and rivalries, heightened by the creation of east European national states and the advent of intense political and economic nationalism, rendered economic co-operation an impossibility despite the obvious need and the heartfelt hopes of business leaders. Above all interwar Europe was dominated by political and ethnic nationalism, invariably strident and jealous, almost always selfish and short-sighted. Perhaps there was a certain inevitability in the eruption of this pent-up nationalism in the aftermath of a war which dissolved the restraints which had contained it for a century. Yet its tactless exercise contributed to the development, once the new and inadequate restraints of the Versailles Treaty had also dissolved, of the most virulent and dangerous nationalism of all, that of Nazi Germany under Adolf Hitler.

In restrospect much of the instability of the interwar international structure arose from Germany's consistent refusal to accept her existing circumstances. Without German revisionism to disturb the tranquillity of Europe, many of the other problems would probably have dissipated in time as new nations became more mature and their minorities partially assimilated. But the advent of Hitler indicated that Germany's discontent was now being translated into the will to act forcibly. Most west European leaders knew well how fragile the foundation of peace was and recognised at once that Hitler intended to smash it. They knew, too, that only the western democracies, possibly in reluctant combination with the distrusted Soviet regime, had sufficient power potential to counter this obvious threat to peace. Yet they were unable to meet the threat because public opinion had swallowed the comforting illusion that peace could be ensured by collective security entrusted to a limping League of disarmed nations. Given Adolf Hitler in full control of Europe's most powerful and most dissatisfied nation, it certainly could not, if ever it could have been. It is not only ironic but also tragic that, aside from Hitler's aggressive aims and his single-minded pursuit of them, the major factor forcing Europe toward the ultimate inevitability of the Second World War was the intense yearning of the western democracies for peace, however illusory.

Chronological Table

1915	18 January	Japan's 21 Demands on China
	26 April	Allied–Italian Treaty of London
	25 May	Sino-Japanese agreements
	24 October	McMahon Pledge to Sharif Hussein
1916	16 May	Sykes–Picot agreement on Middle East
1917	2 November	Balfour Declaration on Palestine
	7 November	Lenin's *coup* in Russia
1918	8 January	Wilson's Fourteen Points
	17 February	British forces land in Transcaucasus
	3 March	Russo-German Treaty of Brest-Litovsk
	5 April	Japanese occupy Vladivostok
	23 June	British forces land at Murmansk
	4 October	Germany requests an armistice
	30 October	Turkish unconditional surrender
	3 November	Austro-Hungarian Armistice
	6 November	Pre-Armistice agreement with Germany
	11 November	German Armistice
1919	18 January	Paris Peace Conference opens
	14 February	League of Nations Covenant approved
	4 March	Comintern founded at Moscow
	24 March	Council of Four begins
	28 March	Hungary invades Slovakia
	29 March	China leaves Peace Conference
	7 May	Versailles Treaty presented to Germany
	28 June	Versailles Treaty signed
		First Minorities Treaty
	10 September	Treaty of Saint-Germain-en-Laye with Austria
	12 September	D'Annunzio seizes Fiume
	12 October	British evacuate Murmansk
	27 November	Treaty of Neuilly with Bulgaria
1920	10 January	Versailles Treaty enters into force
	2 February	Russo-Estonian peace treaty of Tartu (Dorpat)
	16 March	Allies occupy Constantinople

	19 March	Final U.S. Senate defeat of Versailles Treaty
	4 April	France occupies Frankfurt
	18–26 April	San Remo Conference
	25 April	Polish offensive against Russia
	4 June	Treaty of Trianon with Hungary
	6 July	Russian offensive against Poland
	12 July	Russo-Lithuanian peace treaty of Moscow
	16 July	Spa Protocol on reparations
	10 August	Treaty of Sèvres with Turkey
	11 August	Russo-Latvian peace treaty of Riga
	14 August	Czech–Yugoslav alliance
	14–16 August	Poles defeat Russians at Warsaw
	7 September	Franco-Belgian military convention
	9 October	Poland seizes Vilna
	14 October	Russo-Finnish peace treaty of Tartu
	28 October	Bessarabian Accord
	12 November	Italo-Yugoslav treaty of Rapallo
1921	19 February	Franco-Polish alliance
	3 March	Polish–Romanian pact against Russia
	8 March	Entente occupation of Düsseldorf
	16 March	Anglo-Soviet trade agreement
	18 March	Russo-Polish peace treaty of Riga
	20 March	Upper Silesian plebiscite
	27 March	Habsburg *coup* in Hungary fails
	5 May	London Schedule of Payments
	5 June	Czech–Romanian alliance
	7 June	Yugoslav–Romanian alliance
	25 August	U.S.–German peace treaty of Berlin
	21–25 October	Habsburg *coup* in Hungary fails
	12 November	Washington Conference opens
	6 December	Anglo-Irish peace agreement
1922	6–13 January	Cannes Conference
	6 February	Five Power Treaty on Naval Limitations
		Nine Power Treaty on China
		Four Power Treaty on Pacific Islands
	15 March	Russo-German military agreement
	10 April–	Genoa Conference
	19 May	
	16 April	Russo-German treaty of Rapallo
	1 August	Balfour note on war debts
	4 October	Geneva Protocol for Austrian financial reconstruction
	11 October	Mudanya armistice ends Chanak crisis

	25 October	Japanese evacuate Vladivostok
	26 December	Reparations Commission declares German timber default
1923	9 January	Reparations Commission declares German coal default
	10 January	Lithuania occupies Memel
	11 January	Ruhr occupation begins
	19 January	German passive resistance begins
	30 January	Greco-Turkish convention on minorities exchange
	14 July	Treaty of Lausanne with Turkey
	31 August	Italy occupies Corfu
	12 September	Draft Treaty of Mutual Assistance
	17 September	Italy seizes Fiume
	26 September	German passive resistance ends
	20 November	German currency stabilised
1924	25 January	Franco-Czech alliance
	27 January	Italo-Yugoslav treaty of Rome
	1 February	Britain recognises Soviet government
	9 April	Dawes Plan issued
	18 April	League reorganises Hungarian finances
	5 July	Britain rejects Draft Treaty of Mutual Assistance
	16 July– 16 August	London Reparations Conference
	2 October	Geneva Protocol for Pacific Settlement of International Disputes
	25 October	Zinoviev letter published
1925	15 February	I.M.C.C. Final Report
	10 March	Britain rejects Geneva Protocol
	27 August	Last French troops leave the Ruhr
	16 October	Locarno treaties initialled
	22 October	Greece invades Bulgaria
	1 December	Locarno treaties signed
1926	31 January	First Rhineland zone evacuated
	17 March	Brazil blocks German League entry
	26 March	Polish–Romanian guarantee treaty
	24 April	Russo-German treaty of Berlin
	10 June	Franco-Romanian friendship treaty
	12 June	Brazil leaves the League
	17 August	Greco-Yugoslav friendship treaty
	10 September	Germany enters the League
	11 September	Spain leaves the League
	16 September	Italo-Romanian friendship treaty

	17 September	Thoiry talks
	26 September	International Steel Agreement
	3–6 October	First Pan-European Congress, Vienna
	27 November	Italo-Albanian treaty of Tirana
1927	31 January	I.M.C.C. abolished
	25 February	British forces mass at Shanghai
	5 April	Italo-Hungarian friendship treaty
	2–23 May	World Economic Conference, Geneva
	27 May	Britain breaks relations with Russia
	20 June– 4 August	Geneva Naval Conference
	11 November	Franco-Yugoslav treaty of understanding
	10 December	Polish–Lithuanian state of war ends
1928	27 August	Kellogg–Briand Pact
	16 September	Geneva communiqué on Rhineland and reparations
1929	9 February	Litvinov Protocol
	11 February	Lateran Accords
	7 June	Young Report issued
	31 August	Hague Conference Protocol on Young Plan
	3 October	Anglo-Russian relations restored
	29 October	New York Stock Exchange collapse
	13 November	Bank for International Settlements established
	30 November	Second Rhineland zone evacuated
1930	3–20 January	Second Hague Conference
	18 February– 24 March	Geneva tariff conference
	22 April	London Naval Treaty
	17 May	Young Plan into force
		Briand memo on United States of Europe
	30 June	Last Rhineland zone evacuated
	14 September	German Reichstag elections (107 Nazis)
1931	20 March	Reichstag appropriation for Cruiser B
	21 March	Austro-German customs union announced
	11 May	Austrian Creditanstalt fails
	19 May	*Deutschland* launched
	20 June	Hoover Moratorium proposed
	11 August	London Protocol on Hoover Moratorium
	5 September	P.C.I.J. ruling on Austro-German customs union
	18 September	Mukden incident
	21 September	Britain abandons Gold Standard
	11 December	Statute of Westminster

1932	7 January	Stimson note on non-recognition
	21 January	Russo-Finnish non-aggression pact
	22 January	Second Russian five-year plan
	28 January	Sino-Japanese clash at Shanghai
	2 February	Geneva Disarmament Conference opens
	5 February	Russo-Latvian non-aggression pact
	9 March	Manchukuo proclaimed
	11 March	League adopts non-recognition
	4 May	Russo-Estonian non-aggression pact
	16 June– 9 July	Lausanne reparations conference
	21 July– 20 August	Imperial Economic Conference, Ottawa
	25 July	Russo-Polish non-aggression pact
	29 November	Russo-French non-aggression pact
1933	30 January	Hitler becomes German Chancellor
	16 February	Little Entente Pact of Organisation
	24 February	League adopts Lytton Report
	27 March	Japan leaves the League
	31 May	Sino-Japanese truce of T'ang-Ku
	12 June– 27 July	World Economic Conference, London
	15 July	Four Power Pact signed at Rome
	14 October	Germany leaves League and Disarmament Conference
1934	26 January	German–Polish non-aggression pact
	18 September	Russia enters League
1935	2 May	Russo-French mutual assistance treaty
	16 May	Russo-Czech mutual assistance treaty
1936	7 March	Hitler remilitarises Rhineland and denounces Locarno pacts
1937	7 July	Sino-Japanese war begins
	5 October	Roosevelt's quarantine speech

Bibliography

THE following lists exclude unpublished materials.

I. DOCUMENTS AND OFFICIAL PUBLICATIONS

Belgium, Académie Royale de Belgique, *Documents Diplomatiques Belges, 1920–1940*, 5 vols (Brussels, 1964–6).

FRITZ BERBER, *Locarno, eine Dokumentensammlung* (Berlin, 1936).

PHILIP M. BURNETT, *Reparations at the Paris Peace Conference from the Standpoint of the American Delegation*, 2 vols (New York, 1940).

JANE DEGRAS (ed.), *The Communist International, 1919–1943, Documents*, 3 vols (London, 1956–65).

——, *Soviet Documents on Foreign Policy*, 3 vols (London, 1951–3).

XENIA J. EUDIN, *et al*, *Soviet Foreign Policy, 1928–1934, Documents and Materials*, 2 vols (University Park, Penna, 1966–7).

——, *Soviet Russia and the East, 1920–1927* (Palo Alto, Cal., 1957).

——, *Soviet Russia and the West, 1920–1927* (Palo Alto, Cal., 1957).

France, Ministère des Affaires Étrangères, *Documents Diplomatiques* (various).

Germany, *Akten der Reichskanzlei, Das Kabinett Cuno* (*et al.*), multi-vol. and continuing (Boppard am Rhein, 1968–).

——, *Akten zur Deutschen Auswärtigen Politik, 1918–1945*, Series B, multi-vol. and continuing (Göttingen, 1966–).

——, Ministerium für Auswärtige Augelegenheiten, *Locarno-Konferenz, 1925; Eine Dokumentensammlung* (Berlin, 1962).

——, Peace Delegation, *Comments by the German Delegation on the Conditions of Peace* (Berlin, 1919).

Great Britain, Foreign Office, *British and Foreign State Papers*, multi-vol. and continuing (London, 1814–).

——, ——, *Documents on British Foreign Policy, 1919–1939*, multi-vol. and continuing (London, 1958–).

——, Parliament, *Command Papers*, various, too numerous to list.

RUTH B. HENIG (ed.), *The League of Nations* (New York, 1974).

FRED L. ISRAEL, *Major Peace Treaties of Modern History, 1648–1967*, 4 vols (New York, 1967).

Italy, Commissione per la Publicazione dei Documenti Diplomatici, *I Documenti Diplomatici Italiani*, 6th and 7th Series, multi-vol. and continuing (Rome, 1952–).

A. DE LA PRADELLE (ed.), *La Documentation Internationale: La Paix de Versailles*, 12 vols (Paris, 1929–39).

League of Nations, *Official Journal* (Geneva, 1920–40).

——, *Treaty Series*, 205 vols (Geneva, 1920–46).

PAUL MANTOUX, *Paris Peace Conference, 1919, Proceedings of the Council of Four*, 2 vols (Geneva, 1964).

DAVID HUNTER MILLER, *The Drafting of the Covenant*, 2 vols (New York, 1928).

——, *My Diary at the Conference of Paris with Documents*, 21 vols (privately printed, n.d.).

EDGAR B. NIXON (ed.), *Franklin D. Roosevelt and Foreign Affairs*, 3 vols (Cambridge, Mass., 1969).

J. R. H. O'REGAN *The German War of 1914* (London, 1915).

Poland, Ministry of Foreign Affairs, *Official Documents Concerning Polish–German and Polish–Soviet Relations, 1933–1939. The Polish White Book* (London, n.d.).

Reparation Commission, *Official Documents*, 23 vols (London, 1922–30).

LEONARD SHAPIRO (ed.), *Soviet Treaty Series*, 2 vols (Washington, 1950).

United States, Department of State, *Papers Relating to the Foreign Relations of the United States* (Washington, annual); *Japan, 1921–1941*, 2 vols (Washington, 1943); *The Lansing Papers, 1914–1920*, 2 vols (Washington, 1939–40); *1918, Russia*, 4 vols (Washington, 1931–7); *The Paris Peace Conference, 1919*, 13 vols (Washington, 1942–7).

——, 67th Congress, Second Session, Senate Document No. 126, *Conference on the Limitation of Armament* (Washington, 1922).

J. W. WHEELER-BENNETT (ed.), *Documents on International Affairs, 1928*, et seq., (London, annual, 1929–).

THOMAS WOODROW WILSON, *War and Peace: Presidential Messages, Addresses, and Public Papers, 1917–1924*, 2 vols (New York, 1927).

2. DIARIES, LETTERS AND MEMOIRS

MAJ.-GEN. HENRY T. ALLEN, *My Rhineland Journal* (London, 1924).

CARL BERGMAN, *The History of Reparations* (London, 1927).

STEPHEN BONSAL, *Suitors and Suppliants: The Little Nations at Versailles* (New York, 1946).

——, *Unfinished Business* (Garden City, N.Y., 1944).

MAJOR.-GEN. SIR CHARLES E. CALLWELL, *Field Marshal Sir Henry Wilson, His Life and Diaries*, 2 vols (London, 1927).

E. A. R. G. CECIL (VISCOUNT CECIL OF CHELWOOD), *A Great Experiment* (London, 1941).

CHARLES G. DAWES, *A Journal of Reparations* (London, 1939).

RAYMOND B. FOSDICK, *Letters on the League of Nations* (Princeton, N.J., 1966).

ANDRÉ FRANÇOIS-PONCET, *De Versailles à Potsdam, la France et le Problème Allemand Contemporain, 1919–1945* (Paris, 1948).

GASTON FURST, *De Versailles aux experts* (Nancy, 1927).

COL. MAURICE HANKEY (BARON HANKEY), *Diplomacy by Conference* (London, 1946).

——, *The Supreme Control at the Paris Peace Conference, 1919* (London, 1963).

SIR JAMES HEADLAM-MORLEY, *Memoir of the Paris Peace Conference, 1919* (London, 1972).

GUSTAV HILGER AND ALFRED G. MEYER, *The Incompatible Allies: German–Soviet Relations, 1918–1941* (New York, 1953).

ADMIRAL NICHOLAS HORTHY, *Mémoires* (Paris, 1954).

PAUL HYMANS, *Mémoires*, 2 vols (Brussels, 1958).

EMERY KELEN, *Peace in their Time* (London, 1964).

ROBERT LANSING, *The Big Four and Others of the Peace Conference* (New Haven, Conn., 1965).

——, *The Peace Negotiations, A Personal Narrative* (Boston, Mass., 1921).

DAVID LLOYD GEORGE, *Memoirs of the Peace Conference*, 2 vols (New Haven, Conn., 1939).

——, *The Truth about Reparations and War Debts* (London, 1932).

SIR ANDREW MCFADYEAN, *Reparation Reviewed* (London, 1930).

BRIG.-GEN. JOHN H. MORGAN, *Assize of Arms: Being the Story of the Disarmament of Germany and her Rearmament* (London, 1945).

HAROLD NICOLSON, *Peacemaking, 1919* (London, 1933).

SIR CHARLES PETRIE, *The Life and Letters of the Right Honourable Sir Austen Chamberlain*, 2 vols (London, 1940).

GEORGE A. RIDDELL (BARON RIDDELL), *Lord Riddell's Intimate Diary of the Peace Conference and After, 1918–1923* (London, 1933).

J. A. SALTER (BARON SALTER), *Memoirs of a Public Servant* (London, 1961).

HJALMAR SCHACHT, *Confessions of the 'Old Wizard': Autobiography* (Boston, Mass., 1956).

CHARLES SEYMOUR (ed.), *The Intimate Papers of Colonel House*, 4 vols (London, 1926–8).

——, *Letters from the Paris Peace Conference* (New Haven, Conn., 1965).

HENRY L. STIMSON, *The Far Eastern Crisis: Recollections and Observations* (New York, 1936).

ERIC SUTTON (ed.), *Gustav Stresemann: His Diaries, Letters, and Papers*, 3 vols (London, 1937).

PAUL TIRARD, *La France sur le Rhin: Douze Années d'Occupation Rhénane* (Paris, 1930).

EDGAR VINCENT (VISCOUNT D'ABERNON), *An Ambassador of Peace: Lord D'Abernon's Diary*, 3 vols (London, 1929).

THOMAS WOODROW WILSON, *Woodrow Wilson, Life and Letters*, 8 vols, (London, 1939).

3. SECONDARY WORKS

RENÉ ALBRECHT-CARRIÉ, *Italy at the Paris Peace Conference* (New York, 1938).

WILLIAM S. ALLEN, *The Nazi Seizure of Power* (Chicago, 1965).

N. ALMOND AND R. LUTZ, *The Treaty of Saint-Germain* (Palo Alto, Cal., 1935).

GEORGE ANTONIUS, *The Arab Awakening* (New York, 1939).

THOMAS BAILEY, *Woodwow Wilson and the Lost Peace* (New York, 1944).

RAY STANNARD BAKER, *Woodrow Wilson and World Settlement*, 3 vols (New York, 1922).

JACQUES BARDOUX, *Lloyd George et la France* (Paris, 1923).

JAMES BARROS, *The Corfu Incident of 1923* (Princeton, N.J., 1965).

——, *The League of Nations and the Great Powers* (Oxford, 1970).

RONALD P. BARSTON, *The Other Powers* (New York, 1973).

EDWARD M. BENNETT, *Germany and the Diplomacy of the Financial Crisis, 1931* (Cambridge, Mass., 1962).

DANIEL A. BINCHY, *Church and State in Fascist Italy* (New York, 1941).

PAUL BIRDSALL, *Versailles Twenty Years After* (London, 1941).

K. D. BRACHER, *The German Dictatorship* (New York, 1970).

JOHN BRADLEY, *Allied Intervention in Russia, 1917–1920* (New York, 1968).

JULIUS BRAUNTHAL, *History of the International*, 2 vols (New York, 1967).

BOHDAN B. BUDOROWYCZ, *Polish–Soviet Relations, 1932–1939* (New York, 1963).

EMILE CAMMAERTS, *Albert of Belgium, Defender of Right* (London, 1935).

DAVID CARLTON, *MacDonald versus Henderson: The Foreign Policy of the Second Labour Government* (New York, 1970).

E. H. CARR, *A History of Soviet Russia: The Bolshevik Revolution, 1917–1923*, 3 vols (London, 1950–53).

F. L. CARSTEN, *Revolution in Central Europe, 1918–1919* (Berkeley, Cal., 1972).

GWENDOLEN M. CARTER, *The British Commonwealth and International Security: the Role of the Dominions, 1919–1939* (Toronto, 1947).

LEWIS CARTER, et al., *The Zinoviev Letter* (London, 1967).

ALAN CASSELS, *Mussolini's Early Diplomacy* (Princeton, N.J., 1970).

INIS L. CLAUDE Jr, *Swords into Plowshares: the Problems and Progress of International Organization* (New York, 1971 ed.)

GORDON A. CRAIG AND FELIX GILBERT (eds), *The Diplomats, 1919–1939* (Princeton, N.J., 1953).

FERDINAND CZERNIN, *Versailles, 1919* (New York, 1965 ed.).

NORMAN DAVIES, *White Eagle, Red Star: The Polish–Soviet War, 1919–20* (New York, 1972).

FRANCIS DEÁK, *Hungary at the Paris Peace Conference* (New York, 1942).

ROMAN DEBICKI, *Foreign Policy of Poland, 1919–1939* (New York, 1962).

PETER DENNIS, *Decision by Default: Peacetime Conscription and British Defence, 1919–39* (Durham, N.C., 1972).

IAN M. DRUMMOND, *British Economic Policy and the Empire, 1919–39* (London, 1972).

ERICH EYCK, *A History of the Weimar Republic*, 2 vols (Cambridge, Mass., 1962).

JEAN-CLAUDE FAVEZ, *Le Reich devant l'Occupation Franco-Belge de la Ruhr en 1923* (Geneva, 1969).

R. H. FERRELL, *The American Secretaries of State and their Diplomacy*, XI, *Frank B. Kellogg, Henry L. Stimson* (New York, 1963).

——, *Peace in their Time* (New Haven, Conn., 1952).

RUSSELL FIFIELD, *Woodrow Wilson and the Far East* (New York, 1952).

LOUIS FISCHER, *Russia's Road from Peace to War: Soviet Foreign Relations, 1917–1941* (New York, 1969).

INGA FLOTO, *Colonel House in Paris: A Study of American Policy at the Paris Peace Conference, 1919* (Åarhus, Denmark, 1973).

MICHAEL G. FRY, *Illusions of Security: North Atlantic Diplomacy, 1918–1922* (Toronto, 1972).

HANS GATZKE (ed.), *European Diplomacy between Two Wars* (Chicago, 1972).

——, *Stresemann and the Rearmament of Germany* (Baltimore, Md, 1954).

LAURENCE E. GELFAND, *The Inquiry: American Preparations for Peace, 1917–1919* (New Haven, Conn., 1963).

CHARLES A. GULICK, *Austria from Habsburg to Hitler*, 2 vols (Berkeley, Cal., 1948).

SIR JAMES W. HEADLAM-MORLEY, *Studies in Diplomatic History* (London, 1930).

PAUL C. HELMREICH, *From Paris to Sèvres* (Columbus, Ohio, 1973).

EDOUARD HERRIOT, *The United States of Europe* (London, 1930).

ERVIN HEXNER, *The International Steel Cartel* (Chapel Hill, N.C., 1943).

YAMOTO ICHIHASHI, *The Washington Conference and After* (Palo Alto, Cal., 1928).

JON JACOBSON, *Locarno Diplomacy* (Princeton, N.J., 1972).

WILLIAM M. JORDAN, *Great Britain, France, and the German Problem, 1918–1939* (London, 1943).

GEORGE F. KENNAN, *The Decision to Intervene* (Princeton, N.J., 1958).

——, *Russia and the West under Lenin and Stalin* (Boston, Mass., 1961).

JOHN MAYNARD KEYNES, *The Economic Consequences of the Peace* (London, 1919).

CHARLES P. KINDLEBERGER, *The World in Depression, 1919–1939* (London, 1973).

JERE C. KING, *Foch versus Clemenceau; France and German Dismemberment, 1918–1919* (Cambridge, Mass., 1960).

SIR IVONE KIRKPATRICK, *Mussolini: a Study in Power* (New York, 1964).

J. KORBEL, *Poland between East and West* (Princeton, N.J., 1963).

WARREN F. KUEHL, *Seeking World Order: The United States and International Organization to 1920* (Nashville, Tenn., 1969).

IVO LEDERER, *Yugoslavia at the Paris Peace Conference* (New Haven, Conn., 1963).

N. GORDON LEVIN Jr, *Woodrow Wilson and World Politics* (London, 1968).

BERNARD LEWIS, *The Emergence of Modern Turkey* (London, 1968 ed.)

ARTHUR S. LINK, *Wilson the Diplomatist* (Baltimore, Md, 1957).

ALMA LUCKAU, *The German Delegation at the Paris Peace Conference* (New York, 1941).

C. A. MACARTNEY, *Hungary and her Successors, 1919–1937* (London, 1937).

—— AND A. W. PALMER, *Independent Eastern Europe* (London, 1966).

MAXWELL H. H. MACARTNEY AND PAUL CREMONA, *Italy's Foreign and Colonial Policy, 1914–1937* (New York, 1938).

ROBERT MACHRAY, *The Little Entente* (London, 1929).

——, *The Struggle for the Danube and the Little Entente, 1929–38* (London, 1938).

PETER MANSFIELD, *The Ottoman Empire and its Successors* (London, 1973).

ETIENNE MANTOUX, *The Carthaginian Peace, or the Economic Consequences of Mr. Keynes* (Oxford, 1946).

F. S. MARSTON, *The Peace Conference of 1919: Organization and Procedure* (London, 1944).

LAURENCE W. MARTIN, *Peace without Victory* (New Haven, Conn., 1958).

ARNO MAYER, *Politics and Diplomacy of Peacemaking: Containment and Counterrevolution at Versailles, 1918–1919* (New York, 1967).

KERMIT E. MCKENZIE, *Comintern and World Revolution, 1928–1943* (New York, 1964).

W. N. MEDLICOTT, *British Foreign Policy since Versailles* (London, 1968 ed.).

RICHARD H. MEYER, *Banker's Diplomacy* (New York, 1970).

DAVID HUNTER MILLER, *The Geneva Protocol* (New York, 1925).

LEONARD O. MOSLEY, *Curzon, the End of an Epoch* (London, 1960).

DENYS P. MYERS, *The Reparations Settlement* (Boston, Mass., 1929).

HAROLD NELSON, *Land and Power: British and Allied Policy on Germany's Frontiers, 1916–19* (Toronto, 1963).

A. J. NICHOLLS, *Weimar and the Rise of Hitler* (London, 1968).

HAROLD NICOLSON, *Curzon: the Last Phase, 1919–1925* (London, 1934).

IAN H. NISH, *Alliance in Decline: A Study in Anglo-Japanese Relations, 1908–1923* (London, 1972).

PHILIP J. NOEL-BAKER, *The Geneva Protocol for the Pacific Settlement of International Disputes* (London, 1925).

GÜNTHER NOLLAU, *International Communism and World Revolution* (New York, 1961).

VÉRA OLIVOVÁ, *The Doomed Democracy: Czechoslovakia in a Disrupted Europe, 1914–1938* (London, 1972)

JOSÉ ORTEGA Y GASSET, *The Revolt of the Masses* (New York, 1930).

FRANK OWEN, *Tempestuous Journey: Lloyd George, his Life and Times* (New York, 1955).

GAINES POST, Jr, *The Civil–Military Fabric of Weimar Foreign Policy* (Princeton, N.J., 1973).

PIERRE RAIN, *L'Europe de Versailles, 1919–1939* (Paris, 1945).

GEORGE VON RAUCH, *The Baltic States: the Years of Independence: Estonia, Latvia, Lithuania, 1917–1940* (Berkeley, Cal., 1974).

HANS ROOS, *A History of Modern Poland* (New York, 1966).

STEPHEN W. ROSKILL, *Hankey: Man of Secrets*, 3 vols (London, 1970–74).

——, *Naval Policy between the Wars*, vol. 1 (London, 1968).

ROBERT L. ROTHSTEIN, *Alliances and Small Powers* (New York, 1968).

J. S. ROUCEK, *Balkan Politics: International Relations in No Man's Land* (Palo Alto, Cal., 1948).

HARRY RUDIN, *Armistice, 1918* (New Haven, Conn., 1944).

MICHAEL SALEWSKI, *Entwaffnung und Militärkontrolle in Deutschland, 1919–1927* (Munich, 1966).

SIR J. ARTHUR SALTER, *Personality in Politics: Studies of Contemporary Statesmen* (London, 1947).

GODFREY SCHEELE, *The Weimar Republic* (London, 1956).

BERNADOTTE E. SCHMITT (ed.), *Poland* (Berkeley, Cal., 1945).

GERHARD SCHULZ, *Revolutions and Peace Treaties, 1917–1920* (New York, 1972).

CHRISTOPHER SETON-WATSON, *Italy from Liberalism to Fascism, 1870–1925* (London, 1967).

HUGH SETON-WATSON, *Eastern Europe between the Wars, 1918–1941* (Cambridge, England, 1945).

J. T. SHOTWELL AND MARINA SALVIN, *Lessons on Security and Disarmament* (New York, 1949).

SARA SMITH, *The Manchurian Crisis* (New York, 1948).

JÜRGEN SPENZ, *Die Diplomatische Vorgeschichte des Beitritts Deutschlands zum Völkerbund, 1924–1926* (Göttingen, 1966).

GEORGES SUAREZ, *Briand, sa vie, son oeuvre*, 6 vols (Paris, 1941–52).

STANLEY SUVAL, *The Anschluss Question in the Weimar Era* (Baltimore, Md, 1974).

ANDRÉ TARDIEU, *The Truth about the Treaty* (Indianapolis, Ind., 1921).

EDMOND TAYLOR, *The Fall of the Dynasties: the Collapse of the Old Order, 1905–1922* (New York, 1963).

HAROLD W. V. TEMPERLEY, *A History of the Peace Conference of Paris*, 6 vols (London, 1920–24).

CHRISTOPHER THORNE, *The Limits of Foreign Policy* (London, 1972).

SETH P. TILLMAN, *Anglo-American Relations at the Paris Peace Conference of 1919* (Princeton, N.J., 1961).

A. J. TOYNBEE (ed.), *Survey of International Affairs, 1920–1923* (et seq.), annual (London, 1927–).

HENRY A. TURNER Jr, *Stresemann and the Politics of the Weimar Republic* (Princeton, N.J., 1956).

ADAM B. ULAM, *Expansion and Coexistence: The History of Soviet Foreign Policy, 1917–1967* (New York, 1968).

RICHARD ULLMAN, *Anglo-Soviet Relations, 1917–1921*, 3 vols (Princeton, N.J., 1961–7).

ROBERT WAITE, *Vanguard of Nazism* (Cambridge, Mass., 1952).

FRANCIS P. WALTERS, *A History of the League of Nations* (London, 1952).

SARAH WAMBAUGH, *Plebiscites since the World War* (Washington D.C., 1933).

PIOTR WANDYCZ, *France and her Eastern Allies, 1919–1925* (Minneapolis, Minn., 1962).

——, *Soviet–Polish Relations, 1917–1921* (Cambridge, Mass., 1969).

ÉTIENNE WEILL-RAYNALL, *Les Réparations allemandes et la France,* 3 vols (Paris, 1947).

GERHARD WEINBERG, *The Foreign Policy of Hitler's Germany* (Chicago, 1970).

K. C. WHEARE, *The Statute of Westminster and Dominion Status* (New York, 1938).

J. W. WHEELER-BENNETT, *Hindenburg: The Wooden Titan* (London, 1936).

——, *The Nemesis of Power: The German Army in Politics, 1918–1945* (New York, 1964).

——, *The Pipe Dream of Peace* (London, 1935).

——, *The Wreck of Reparations* (London, 1933).

ANN WILLIAMS, *Britain and France in the Middle East and North Africa, 1914–1967* (London, 1968).

BRUCE WILLIAMS, *State Security and the League of Nations* (Baltimore, Md, 1927).

WESTEL W. WILLOUGHBY, *The Sino-Japanese Controversy and the League of Nations* (New York, 1935).

HENRY R. WINKLER, *The League of Nations Movement in Great Britain, 1914–1919* (New Brunswick, N.J., 1952).

ELIZABETH WISKEMANN, *Czechs and Germans* (London, 1967 ed.)

——, *Fascism in Italy* (London, 1969).

J. W. WUORINEN, *Scandinavia* (Englewood Cliffs, N.J., 1965).

Z. N. ZEINE, *The Struggle for Arab Independence* (Beirut, 1960).

Z. A. B. ZEMAN, *The Break-up of the Habsburg Empire, 1914–1918* (London, 1961).

LUDWIG ZIMMERMANN, *Deutsche Aussenpolitik in der Ära der Weimarer Republik* (Göttingen, 1958).

ALFRED E. ZIMMERN, *League of Nations and the Rule of Law, 1918–1935* (New York, 1939).

BARON PIERRE VAN ZUYLEN, *Les Mains libres: Politique extérieure de la Belgique, 1914–1940* (Brussels, 1950).

4. PERIODICALS

(a) *Articles Cited*

GEORGE A. GRÜN, 'Locarno, idea and reality', *International Affairs* (October, 1955).

F. G. STAMBROOK, ' "*Das Kind*" – Lord D'Abernon and the origins of the Locarno Pact', *Central European History* (September, 1968).

Le Temps (Paris, 4 May 1922 et seq.).

The Times (London, 25 October 1924).

T.R.B. (RICHARD L. STROUT), 'The tarnished age', *New Republic* (26 October 1974).

(b) *Generally Useful Journals.*

Central European History.
French Historical Studies.
International Affairs.
Journal of British Studies.
Journal of Central European Affairs.
Journal of Contemporary History.
Journal of Modern History.
Mid-America.
The Slavonic and East European Review.

(c) *Generally Useful Newspapers.*

The Christian Science Monitor (Boston, Mass., and international editions).
The Manchester Guardian.
The New York Herald Tribune.
The New York Times (indexed).
Le Temps (Paris).
The Times (London) (indexed).

Notes and References

ABBREVIATIONS

CAB 2/–, CAB 23/–	Cabinet Papers, Public Record Office (P.R.O.), London
Cmd.	Parliamentary Command Papers, London
DBFP	Foreign Office, *Documents on British Foreign Policy, 1919–1939*, London
DD	Ministère des Affaires Étrangères, *Documents Diplomatiques*, various, Paris
DDB	Académie Royale de Belgique, *Documents Diplomatiques Belges, 1920–1940*, Brussels
DIA	Royal Institute of International Affairs, *Documents on International Affairs*, London, annual
F.O. 371/–	Foreign Office files, Public Record Office (P.R.O.), London
FRUS	Department of State, *Papers Relating to the Foreign Relations of the United States*, Washington, annual
FRUS PPC	Department of State, *The Paris Peace Conference, 1919*, Washington
Hymans/–	Papers of Paul Hymans, Archives générales du Royaume, Brussels
S.D.–	Department of State, decimal files, National Archives, Washington
SIA	Royal Institute of International Affairs, *Survey of International Affairs*, London, annual

1. THE PURSUIT OF PEACE

1. On the Inquiry, see Laurence E. Gelfand, *The Inquiry: American Preparations for Peace, 1917–1919* (New Haven, Conn., 1963). In the end most of the experts of the large American delegation came from the Inquiry, not the State Department. A few of them were more influential than some of the plenipotentiaries.

2. On Wilson's vacuity, see Charles Seymour, *Letters from the Paris Peace Conference* (New Haven, Conn., 1965) pp. xxx–xxxii, 10, 20–6; and Robert Lansing, *The Big Four and Others of the Peace Conference* (Boston, Mass., 1921) pp. 40–2.

3. For details, see J. W. Wheeler-Bennett, *The Nemesis of Power: The German Army in Politics, 1918–1945* (New York, 1964).

4. The full annotated text of the Fourteen Points and the subsequent Wilsonian pronouncements may be found in Ferdinand Czernin, *Versailles, 1919* (New York, 1965 ed.) pp. 10–22.

5. The definitive study of the armistice is Harry Rudin, *Armistice, 1918* (New Haven, Conn., 1944).

6. For wartime Czech efforts, see Věra Olivová, *The Doomed Democracy: Czechoslovakia in a Disrupted Europe, 1914–1938* (London, 1972).

7. A convenient summary of the secret treaties may be found in H. W. V. Temperley, *History of the Peace Conference of Paris*, 6 vols (London, 1920) 1.

8. On the Russian situation, see John Bradley, *Allied Intervention in Russia, 1917–1920* (New York, 1968); George F. Kennan, *The Decision to Intervene* (Princeton, N.J., 1958); Richard Ullman, *Anglo-Soviet Relations, 1917–1921*, 3 vols (Princeton, N.J., 1961–7); and Arno Mayer, *Politics and Diplomacy of Peacemaking: Containment and Counterrevolution at Versailles, 1918–1919* (New York, 1967).

9. See Laurence W. Martin, *Peace without Victory* (New Haven, Conn., 1958); N. Gordon Levin, Jr, *Woodrow Wilson and World Politics* (London, 1968); and Harold Nicolson, *Peacemaking, 1919* (London, 1933).

10. On the Shantung question, see Russell Fifield, *Woodrow Wilson and the Far East* (New York, 1952). .

11. See Ann Williams, *Britain and France in the Middle East and North Africa, 1914–1967* (London, 1968) and Peter Mansfield, *The Ottoman Empire and its Successors* (London, 1973).

12. Warren F. Kuehl, *Seeking World Order: The United States and International Organization to 1920* (Nashville, Tenn., 1969) p. 199. On wartime efforts toward international organisation, see Kuehl and also Henry R. Winkler, *The League of Nations Movement in Great Britain, 1914–1919* (New Brunswick, N.J., 1952).

13. The standard work on this subject is Z. A. B. Zeman, *The Break-up of the Habsburg Empire, 1914–1918* (London, 1961).

14. See F. L. Carsten, *Revolution in Central Europe, 1918–1919* (Berkeley, Cal., 1972), and also Bradley. Despite factual errors, Edmond Taylor, *The Fall of the Dynasties: The Collapse of the Old Order, 1905–1922* (New York, 1963) is also useful.

15. While literature on the League of Nations from start to finish tends to be skimpy, David Hunter Miller's *The Drafting of the Covenant*, 2 vols (New York, 1928) provides a detailed participant's account of the deliberations at Paris.

16. On Hankey's important role, see S. W. Roskill's excellent *Hankey: Man of Secrets* (London, 1972) II.

17. Christopher Seton-Watson, *Italy from Liberalism to Fascism, 1870–1925* (London, 1967) p. 537.

18. A detailed and noticeably sympathetic study of the German delegation may be found in Alma Luckau, *The German Delegation at the Paris Peace Conference* (New York, 1941).

19. For the full annotated text of the Treaty of Versailles, see *FRUS PPC*, XIII.

20. A lively and subjective summary of the chief battles of the conference may be found in Thomas Bailey, *Woodrow Wilson and the Lost Peace* (New York, 1944). See also Seth P. Tillman's *Anglo-American Relations at the Paris Peace Conference of 1919* (Princeton, N.J., 1961), and Czernin.

21. This attitude is most fully explored by Martin and by Levin.

22. The definitive study of the formation of the German frontiers is Harold Nelson, *Land and Power: British and Allied Policy on Germany's Frontiers, 1916–19* (Toronto, 1963).

23. Czernin, p. 31.

24. For the 1839 treaties, see *British and Foreign State Papers*, XXVII, 990–1002. For Bethmann–Hollweg's statement, see J. H. R. O'Regan *The German War of 1914* (London, 1915) pp. 49–50.

25. On the impracticality of collective security, see Inis. L. Claude, Jr, *Swords into Plowshares, the Problems and Progress of International Organization* (New York, 1971 ed.) ch. 12.

26. See, among others, Bailey, pp. 312–14, and Eyck, I 80–5.

27. The classic exposition of this view is John Maynard Keynes, *The Economic Consequences of the Peace* (London, 1919). It should be read in conjunction with Étienne Mantoux, *The Carthaginian Peace, or the Economic Consequences of Mr. Keynes* (Oxford, 1946).

28. *FRUS PPC*, II 139, XII 12–13, 16–26, 28–9, 33, 82–6. See also Eyck, I 103; Robert Waite, *Vanguard of Nazism* (Cambridge, Mass., 1952) pp. 6–8; J. W. Wheeler-Bennett, *Hindenburg: The Wooden Titan* (London, 1936) pp. 215–21, 229, 235–8; A. J. Nicholls, *Weimar and the Rise of Hitler* (London, 1968) pp. 53–61.

29. For texts of all four treaties, see Fred L. Israel, *Major Peace Treaties of Modern History, 1648–1967* (New York, 1967) III.

30. On this fear, see Mayer and also Levin.

31. On the Austrian financial collapse and its aftermath, see Charles A. Gulick, *Austria from Habsburg to Hitler*, 2 vols (Berkeley, Cal., 1948) I ch. IX and Stanley Suval, *The Anschluss Question in the Weimar Era* (Baltimore, Md, 1974) ch. XI.

32. On the negotiation of the Treaty of Trianon, see Francis Deák, *Hungary at the Paris Peace Conference* (New York, 1942).

33. See Paul C. Helmreich, *From Paris to Sèvres* (Columbus, Ohio, 1973).

34. *DBFP*, First Series, VIII, 9.

35. For all the texts concerned and an Arab analysis of them, see George Antonius, *The Arab Awakening* (New York, 1939). For more recent studies, see Ann Williams, Mansfield, and Z. N. Zeine, *The Struggle for Arab Independence* (Beirut, 1960).

36. On all three questions, see René Albrecht-Carrié, *Italy at the Paris Peace Conference* (New York, 1938). See also Ivo Lederer, *Yugoslavia at the Paris Peace Conference* (New Haven, Conn., 1963).

37. On the Turkish national movement, see Mansfield and also Bernard Lewis, *The Emergence of Modern Turkey* (London, 1968 ed.). A brief account of the negotiation of the Treaty of Lausanne is provided by Roderic H. Davison, 'Turkish Diplomacy from Mudros to Lausanne,' in Gordon A. Craig and Felix Gilbert (eds), *The Diplomats, 1919–1939* (Princeton, N.J., 1953). The negotiations may also be traced in *DBFP*, First Series, XVIII.

38. For example, Eyck, I 106.

39. For details, see C. A. Macartney, *Hungary and Her Successors, 1919–1937* (London, 1937) and also Macartney and A. W. Palmer, *Independent Eastern Europe* (London, 1966).

40. The late correspondent and Professor Elizabeth Wiskemann so remarked to the author, London, March 1971.

41. Emile Cammaerts, *Albert of Belgium, Defender of Right* (London, 1935) p. 347.

42. For text, see Israel, III.

2. THE EFFORT TO ENFORCE THE PEACE

1. Senator Kenneth Wherry of Nebraska in 1940, as quoted by T.R.B. (Richard L. Strout), 'The tarnished age', *New Republic* (26 Oct 1974) p. 4.

2. Leonard Mosley, *Curzon: The End of an Epoch* (London, 1960) p. 210.

3. José Ortega y Gasset, *The Revolt of the Masses* (New York, 1930, 1957

ed.) p. 55. See also his ch. 14, urging both European union and the necessity for European domination of the world.

4. Maj.-Gen. Sir C. E. Callwell, *Field Marshal Sir Henry Wilson, His Life and Diaries*, 2 vols (London, 1927) II 193.

5. Olivová provides a convenient summary of the central-European ramifications of the Russo-Polish conflict.

6. Summary treatments of the Russo-Polish war and settlement may be found in Hans Roos, *A History of Modern Poland* (New York, 1966), and in Bernadotte E. Schmitt (ed.), *Poland* (Berkeley, Cal., 1945). For more detail, see Piotr Wandycz, *Soviet–Polish Relations, 1917–1921* (Cambridge, Mass., 1969).

7. *FRUS PPC*, XIII 8.

8. *DBFP*, First Series, XVI 864.

9. This nervousness is clearly revealed in Committee of Imperial Defence papers and meetings. See, for example, CAB 2/3, *passim*.

10. *DBFP*, First series, XVI 862.

11. Pierre Rain, *L'Europe de Versailles* (Paris, 1945) p. 141.

12. Sir Robert Vansittart, 'An aspect of International Relations in 1931' (n.d.) p. 29, F.O. 371/15205.

13. See R. Machray, *The Little Entente* (London, 1929). For a brief but more recent and well-researched analysis, see Robert L. Rothstein, *Alliances and Small Powers* (New York, 1968) ch. 4.

14. The Spa negotiations may be traced in *DBFP*, First Series, VIII. The Spa Protocol dividing reparations was published as Cmd. 1615 (London, 1922).

15. Gaston A. Furst, *De Versailles aux Experts* (Nancy, 1927) pp. 124–6, 133–4, 346. Also indispensable on any question concerning German reparations is Étienne Weill-Raynall, *Les Réparations Allemandes et la France*, 3 vols (Paris, 1938).

16. The Text of the London Schedule appears in Reparation Commission, *Official Documents* (London, 1922) I. The London Conference may be traced in *DBFP*, First Series, XV.

17. For the Franco-Belgian negotiations, see *DDB*, I. For the eastern alliances, see Piotr Wandycz, *France and her Eastern Allies, 1919–1925* (Minneapolis, Minn., 1962).

18. The only substantial studies of the Washington Naval Conference are Yamoto Ichihashi, *The Washington Conference and After* (Palo Alto, Cal., 1928), and Ian Nish, *Alliance in Decline: A Study in Anglo-Japanese Relations, 1908–1923* (London, 1972). See also the summary account in *SIA*, 1920–1923. For documents, see Cmd. 1627 (London, 1922); *DD, Conférence de Washington* (Paris, 1923); and especially *FRUS*, 1921, I, and 1922, I. Minutes of meetings may be found in United States, 67th Congress, Second Session, Senate Document No. 126, Conference on the Limitation of Armament (Washington, D.C., 1922).

19. See Georges Suarez, *Briand: sa vie, son œuvre*, 6 vols (Paris, 1941–52) V.

20. Frank Owen, *Tempestuous Journey: Lloyd George, his Life and Times* (New York, 1955) pp. 598–9. On the Anglo-French negotiations, see also Cmd. 2169 (London, 1924) and *DD, Documents Rélatifs aux Négociations Concernant les Garanties de Sécurité....* (Paris, 1924).

21. Jacques Bardoux, *Lloyd George et la France* (Paris, 1923) pp. 18, 19, 30.

22. A thorough study of the Genoa Conference remains to be written. The Rapallo negotiation is summarised in Eyck, I 202–8. For the conference itself, documentary material is contained in Cmd. 1667 (London, 1922); *DD, Conférence Économique Internationale de Gênes* (Paris, 1923); and Jane Degras (ed.), *Soviet Documents on Foreign Policy*, 3 vols (London, 1951–3) I.

23. For details, see Hans Gatzke, 'Russo-German military collaboration

during the Weimar Republic', in *European Diplomacy between Two Wars*, ed. Hans Gatzke (Chicago, 1972). For the memoir of a participant, see Gustav Hilger and Alfred G. Meyer, *The Incompatible Allies, German–Soviet Relations, 1918–1941* (New York, 1953), especially chs VI and VII.

24. *Le Temps* (4 May 1922 et seq.).';

25. See Cmd. 1812 (London, 1923), Cmd. 2258 (London, 1924), and *DD, Demande de Moratorium du Gouvernement Allemand.* . . . (Paris, 1924).

26. F.O. memo (23 Nov. 1922) F.O. 371/7487.

27. Crowe memo (27 Dec. 1922) F.O. 371/7491; Ryan to Lampson (5 Jan 1923) F.O. 371/8626.

28. Commission des Réparations, *Rapport sur les Travaux de la commission des réparations de 1920 à 1922*, 2 vols (Paris, 1923) I 241–7, II 465–88, 430–1.

29. For text, see Cmd. 1812.

30. Godley to War Office (7 Jan. 1923), F.O. 371/8703; Crewe to Curzon (11 Feb. 1923), tel. 173, F.O. 371/8712; Cabinet 10 (23) (15 Feb. 1923) CAB 23/45.

31. *DD, Demande de moratorium* . . ., pp. 93–7; Grahame to Curzon (1 Mar. 1923) tel. 39, F.O. 371/8718; Crewe to Curzon (14 July 1923) no. 680, F.O. 371/8643; Phipps to Tyrrell (8 Sept. 1923), Phipps to Crowe (6 Nov. 1923), Phipps papers (London). To this should be added the substantial evidence from French sources presented by Stephen A. Schuker in his unpublished (but forthcoming) Harvard doctoral dissertation, 'The French Financial Crisis and the Adoption of the Dawes Plan, 1924' (1968) pp. 21, 25, 138.

32. Germany, *Akten der Reichskanzlei, Das Kabinett Cuno* (Boppard am Rhein, 1968) pp. 158–9.

33. Cole to Wigram (30 Jan. 1923) F.O. 371/8709; Ramsbottom to Bennett (24 Aug. 1923) F.O. 371/8651; Board of Trade memo (25 Aug. 1923) F.O. 371/8651.

34. For details, see Nicholls.

35. Ultimately nearly 900 million gold marks or almost £45 million. *FRUS PPC*, XIII, 785.

36. Most published accounts of Rhenish separatism are unreliable. Materials on the subject may be found in F.O. 371/8682–8691, F.O. 371/9770–9776, and Henri Jaspar papers (Brussels), file 235.

37. For text, see Reparations Commission, Official Documents, XIV (London 1927).

38. S.D. 462.00R 296/376.

39. For heavily edited minutes of the technical work of the London Conference, see Cmd. 2258 (London, 1924) and Cmd. 2270 (London, 1924). There were no minutes kept of political discussions. The least inadequate notes were those of Paul Hymans, Belgian Foreign Minister (Hymans/157). Stresemann's exchanges with Berlin are also helpful (German Foreign Ministry microfilm, GFM, 3398/1736 series). For texts of agreements, see Cmd. 2259 (London, 1924).

40. Schuker, p. 366.

3. THE REVISION OF THE PEACE

1. The early negotiations may be traced in *DBFP*, First Series, VIII, XII, and Degras, *Soviet Documents*, I.

2. *The Times* (London, 25 October 1924).

3. On the Comintern, see Julius Braunthal, *History of the International*, 2 vols (New York, 1967) II; Jane Degras (ed.), *The Communist International, 1919–1943:*

Documents, 3 vols (London, 1956–65); and Günther Nollau, *International Communism and World Revolution* (New York, 1961).

4. Nollau, p. 62.

5. The definitive study is James Barros, *The Corfu Incident of 1923: Mussolini and the League of Nations* (Princeton, N.J., 1965).

6. Alan Cassels, *Mussolini's Early Diplomacy* (Princeton, N.J., 1970) pp. 116–19.

7. League of Nations Covenant, Article 15.

8. Very little has been written about the Draft Treaty. However, some material may be found in: Bruce Williams, *State Security and the League of Nations* (Baltimore, Md, 1927); Francis P. Walters, *A History of the League of Nations* (London, 1952); and J. T. Shotwell and Marina Salvin, *Lessons on Security and Disarmament* (New York, 1949).

9. There have been no recent scholarly studies of the Geneva Protocol. The leading contemporary accounts are David Hunter Miller, *The Geneva Protocol* (New York, 1925) and Philip J. Noel-Baker, *The Geneva Protocol for the Pacific Settlement of International Disputes* (London, 1925).

10. Final Report, I.M.C.C., 15 Feb. 1925, F.O. 371/10708.

11. For D'Abernon's role, see F. G. Stambrook, ' "*Das Kind*"–Lord D'Abernon and the origins of the Locarno Pact', *Central European History* (September 1968).

12. A close textual comparison of Cabinet instructions to Stresemann before Locarno (Deutschen Demokratischen Republik, Ministerium für Auswärtige Augelegenheiten, *Locarno-Konferenz, 1925: Eine Dokumentensammlung*, Berlin, 1962, p. 143), British minutes of meetings (F.O. 371/10742), and Vandervelde's reports to Brussels (*DDB*, II) with Stresemann's diary accounts (Eric Sutton (ed.), *Gustav Stresemann: His Diaries, Letters, and Papers*, 3 vols, London, 1937 II, especially pp. 180–201) leads inescapably to this conclusion.

13. For similar assessments based on different evidence, see Annelise Thimme, 'Stresemann and Locarno' in *European Diplomacy between Two Wars*, ed. Hans Gatzke; and also Godfrey Scheele, *The Weimar Republic* (London, 1956). The best book-length studies of Stresemann in English are Henry A. Turner, Jr, *Stresemann and the Politics of the Weimar Republic* (Princeton, N.J., 1956) and Hans Gatzke, *Stresemann and the Rearmament of Germany* (Baltimore, Md, 1954).

14. Unfortunately Suarez, *Briand*, VI, lacks the detail and documentation of the earlier volumes.

15. A major study of Chamberlain's diplomacy is needed. See Sir Charles Petrie, *The Life and Letters of the Right Honourable Sir Austen Chamberlain*, 2 vols (London, 1940) II.

16. For Vandervelde's attitude, which expressed the reaction of socialists everywhere to the Matteotti murder, see Pierre van Zuylen, *Les Mains Libres: Politique Extérieure de la Belgique, 1914–1940* (Brussels, 1950) pp. 215–16. For the Matteotti murder itself, see Elizabeth Wiskemann, *Fascism in Italy* (London, 1969).

17. Sir Ivone Kirkpatrick, *Mussolini: A Study in Power* (New York, 1964) p. 249.

18. Ibid. See also Emery Kelen, *Peace in their Time* (London, 1964) pp. 155–6.

19. Stresemann, *Diaries*, II 228.

20. The negotiations may be traced in F.O. 371/10726–10744.

21. For example, Loc/122/Con, F.O. 371/10744.

22. The only detailed reports of the work of the jurists are to be found in *DDB*, II 316–25.

23. For the public aspect of Locarno, see Kelen, pp. 152–61.

24. For text, see *DDB*, II 345–6.

25. Kelen, pp. 159, 161; van Zuylen, p. 217; Petrie, II, 287–90; Suarez, VI, 129–30.

26. For texts of the Locarno treaties, see Cmd. 2525 (London, 1925).

27. Stresemann, *Diaries*, II 216–17; van Zuylen note, 8 June 1932, Hymans/151.

28. See S. Harrison Thomson, 'Foreign Relations', in Schmitt (ed.), *Poland*, p. 393, and Wandycz, *France and her Eastern Allies*, pp. 361–8.

29. *DDB*, II 213.

30. *DBFP*, Series IA, I 249–51.

31. See George A. Grün, 'Locarno, Idea and Reality', *International Affairs* (October, 1955) pp. 477–85.

32. Turner, p. 216.

33. Minutes of the 1 December 1925 talks are to be found in *DBFP*, Series IA, I.

4. THE YEARS OF ILLUSION

1. On this episode, see James Barros, *The League of Nations and the Great Powers: The Greek–Bulgarian Incident, 1925* (Oxford, 1970).

2. *SIA*, 1926, p. 3.

3. Walters, p. 319.

4. See Erik Lönnroth, 'Sweden: the diplomacy of Östen Undén', in Craig and Gilbert, *The Diplomats*.

5. For text, see *SIA*, 1927.

6. D'Abernon to Foreign Office (11 Aug. 1926) tel. 202, F.O. 371/11270; Cab 33 (26) (19 May 1926) CAB 23/53; Chamberlain to D'Abernon (13 Aug. 1926) tel. 93, FO 371/11270.

7. Suarez, VI 197.

8. Walters, p. 343.

9. Ibid., pp. 342–3.

10. Stephen Bonsal, *Unfinished Business* (Garden City, N.Y., 1944) p. 26.

11. Walters, p. 346.

12. Cf. Stresemann, *Diaries*, III 17–26, and Suarez, VI 219–27. (See p. 171.)

13. On the Belgian and Polish crises, see Richard H. Meyer, *Banker's Diplomacy* (New York, 1970). On Stresemann's eastern manoeuvres, see J. Korbel, *Poland between East and West* (Princeton, N.J., 1963) p. 198. On the French situation, see Jon Jacobson, *Locarno Diplomacy* (Princeton, N.J., 1972) pp. 84–90. While inclining habitually to Stresemann's view, Jacobson provides an invaluable study of the period 1926–9.

14. See Ervin Hexner, *The International Steel Cartel* (Chapel Hill, N.C., 1943).

15. Cassels, p. 390. This is the best study of Mussolini's diplomacy in the 1920s.

16. For text, see *SIA*, 1927.

17. Ibid., 1927.

18. Ibid., 1926.

19. Ibid., 1926.

20. Ibid., 1927.

21. Cassels, p. 313.

22. The negotiations may be traced in *DBFP*, Series IA, III. On Anglo-American naval policy in general and the Geneva conference in particular, see S. W. Roskill, *Naval Policy between the Wars* (London, 1968) I.

23. R. H. Ferrell, *The American Secretaries of State and their Diplomacy*, xi: *Frank B. Kellogg, Henry L. Stimson* (New York, 1963) pp. 171–2.

24. See *DIA*, 1930, for texts. The negotiations may be traced in *DBFP*, Second Series, i. A good account of the London conference may be found in David Carlton, *MacDonald versus Henderson* (New York, 1970) ch. 6.

25. A summary may be found in *SIA*, 1929, pp. 101–8.

26. For text, see *SIA*, 1926.

27. On French–Polish relations in the late twenties, see Roman Debicki, *Foreign Policy of Poland, 1919–1939* (New York, 1962) ch. iii.

28. Korbel, p. 223.

29. Petrie, ii 304.

30. For example, D'Abernon to Foreign Office (25 Sept. 1926) no. 664, F.O. 371/11279; Belgian Army G/S, Study of German Army Budget (25 Feb. 1926) Vicomte Prosper Poullet papers (Brussels), file, 232; *DBFP*, Second Series, ii 585–87.

31. *DBFP*, Series IA, i 381.

32. For text of speech, see *DIA*, 1928.

33. The negotiations may be traced in Cmd. 3109 (1928) and Cmd. 3153 (1928). For final text, see Cmd. 3410 (1929) or *DIA*, 1928. The leading study is R. H. Ferrell, *Peace in their Time* (New Haven, Conn., 1952).

34. *DDB*, ii 528.

35. Stresemann, *Diaries*, iii 383–92; Hymans notes (28 Aug. 1928) Hymans/159; *DDB*, ii 528–30.

36. For text, see *DIA*, 1928, or *DBFP*, Series IA, v 335.

37. The handiest compendium, containing background, text, analysis, account of subsequent events through the Hague Conferences, and conference documents, is Denys P. Myers, *The Reparations Settlement* (Boston, 1929). Carlton, *MacDonald versus Henderson* provides a clear narrative of both the Labour government's response to the Young Plan (ch. 2) and the restoration of relations with Russia (ch. 7).

38. Texts may be found in Myers or *DIA*, 1929.

39. For details, see Nicholls, pp. 136–9, or K. D. Bracher, *The German Dictatorship* (New York, 1970) pp. 160–62.

40. For texts, see Myers or Cmd. 3484 (1930), Cmd. 3763 (1931), and Cmd. 3766 (1931).

41. For text, see *DBFP*, Second Series, i 487–8.

42. Eyck, ii 263–4.

43. *DBFP*, Second Series, i 486.

44. For text, see *DBFP*, Second Series, i 314–24 or *DIA*, 1930.

5. THE CRUMBLING OF ILLUSION

1. Tyrrell to Henderson (14 Jan. 1931) no. 37 (France, Annual Report, 1930) F.O. 371/15646.

2. Granville to Henderson (16 Feb. 1931) no. 150 (Belgium, Annual Report, 1930) F.O. 371/15632.

3. For texts, see *DIA*, 1929.

4. Vansittart memo, 'An Aspect of International Relations in 1931' (n.d.) F.O. 371/15205.

5. For example, Belgian General Staff note (30 July 1930), Comte Charles de Broqueville papers (Brussels), file 650; Belgian Study of German Reichswehr Budget (n.d.) 1931, de Broqueville/648; D'Abernon to Foreign Office

(31 March 1926) no. 178, F.O. 371/11279; Tyrrell to Henderson, no. 661, F.O. 371/15187; *DBFP*, Second Series, II 515-25.

6. Campbell to Vansittart (25 Aug. 1931) pers., F.O. 371/15195.

7. See William S. Allen, *The Nazi Seizure of Power* (Chicago, 1965) pp. 12, 24, 34; Eyck, II 278-79.

8. *DBFP*, Second Series, I 502.

9. See his essay under this title, *SIA*, 1931.

10. Newton to Foreign Office (1 July 1931), tel. 91, F.O. 371/15184.

11. F. G. Stambrook, 'The German-Austrian customs union project of 1931', in *European Diplomacy between Two Wars*, ed. Gatzke, p. 98. The best studies of the Customs Union proposal are Stambrook, Suval and Edward M. Bennett, *Germany and the Diplomacy of the Financial Crisis, 1931* (Cambridge, Mass., 1962), to which this analysis of the events of 1931 owes much. A simplified account of the Austrian crisis may be found in Carlton, ch. 10. The negotiations over the Customs Union may also be traced in *DBFP*, Second Series, II.

12. Bennett, p. 48.

13. For text, see *DIA*, 1931.

14. For text, see *FRUS*, 1931, I 33-5.

15. Tyrrell to Foreign Office (22 June 1931) tel., no number, F.O. 371/15182.

16. Bennett, p. 177.

17. For text, see *DIA*, 1931.

18. For the diplomacy of the Manchurian crisis, see Christopher Thorne, *The Limits of Foreign Policy* (London, 1972), on which this analysis relies heavily. The diplomatic manoeuvres may be traced in *DBFP*, Second Series VIII–XI.

19. See, for instance, *Izvestiia* article (22 Nov. 1931) in Xenia Joukoff Eudin and Robert M. Slusser, *Soviet Foreign Policy, 1928–1934, Documents and Materials* (University Park, Penna, 1966) I 345-7.

20. For text, see *FRUS, Japan, 1931–1941*, I 76.

21. See the portrait by Henry R. Winkler in Craig and Gilbert, *The Diplomats*.

22. Toynbee, *SIA*, 1932, p. 175.

23. Thorne, p. 306.

24. The standard work on the Disarmament Conference is J. W. Wheeler-Bennett, *The Pipe Dream of Peace* (London, 1935). The negotiations may be traced in *DBFP*, Second Series, III–VI.

25. Tyrrell to Foreign Office (13 Jan. 1932) tel. 19S, F.O. 371/16369.

26. On the Austrian situation, see Gulick, II.

27. For text of report, see *DIA*, 1931.

28. Memo on German reparations (31 May 1932) F.O. 371/15910.

29. Tyrrell to Simon (16 Jan. 1933) no. 70 (France, Annual Report, 1932) F.O. 371/17299.

30. Key documents may be found in *DIA*, 1932. The negotiations may be traced in *DBFP*, Second Series, III. The standard work is J. W. Wheeler-Bennett, *The Wreck of Reparations* (London, 1933).

31. *FRUS PPC*, XIII, 409.

32. The curious may consult the *World Almanac, 1974*, p. 510. During the winter war of 1939–40, Finland gained enormous American sympathy as 'the only country to pay its war debts'.

33. Extracts may be found in *DIA*, 1932.

34. Thorne, pp. 332-3.

6. THE END OF ALL ILLUSION

1. Gerhard Weinberg, *The Foreign Policy of Hitler's Germany, Diplomatic Revolution in Europe, 1933–36* (Chicago, 1970) p. 14.

2. Edgar B. Nixon (ed.), *Franklin D. Roosevelt and Foreign Affairs*, 3 vols (Cambridge, Mass., 1969) I 122.

3. On Nazi penetration in Czechoslovakia, see Elizabeth Wiskemann, *Czechs and Germans* (London, 1967 ed.).

4. Rothstein, pp. 149, 152–5. See also Robert Machray, *The Struggle for the Danube and the Little Entente, 1929–38* (London, 1938). Text of the Statute of the Little Entente may be found in *DIA*, 1933.

5. For final text, see *DIA*, 1933. The negotiations may be traced in *DBFP*, Second Series v.

6. For texts, see Poland, Ministry of Foreign Affairs, *Official Documents concerning Polish–German and Polish–Soviet Relations, 1933–1939. The Polish White Book* (London, n.d.) pp. 20–1, and Leonard Shapiro (ed.), *Soviet Treaty Series*, 2 vols (Washington, DC., 1950) II 55–6. For analysis of the German treaty, see Weinberg, ch. 3. On the Russian pact, see Bohdan B. Budorowycz, *Polish–Soviet Relations, 1932–1939* (New York, 1963) ch. 1.

7. Clerk to Simon, 27 Jan. 1934, no. 57 (Belgium, Annual Report, 1933) F.O. 371/17616; Simon to Bland (10 July 1933), F.O. 371/17282; Sargent to Ovey (31 July 1934) F.O. 371/17630; F.O. Memo (30 May 1934) F.O. 371/17630.

8. Minutes of meeting at French Ministry of War (10 March 1933) F.O. 371/16668.

9. Ibid.

10. Tyrrell to Foreign Office (31 Jan. 1933) tel. 20S, F.O. 371/17290; Campbell to Simon (30 Nov. 1934) tel. 130, F.O. 371/17670; Clerk to Eden (13 Nov. 1936) no. 1469, F.O. 371/19860.

11. Thorne, p. 267.

Addendum to note 12, Chapter 4 (page 168)

It is now established that the French account is inaccurate. (Jacques Bariéty, address at Conference on European Security in the Locarno Era, Mars Hill, N.C., 17 Oct. 1975.) It does not necessarily follow, however, that Stresemann's version is reliable.

Index